LORD OF THE FLIES

William Golding

AUTHORED by Jeremy Ross
UPDATED AND REVISED by A. Kimball, December 8, 2006, and A. Kissel,

COVER DESIGN by Table XI Partners LLC
COVER PHOTO by Olivia Verma and © 2005 GradeSaver, LLC

BOOK DESIGN by Table XI Partners LLC

Published by GradeSaver LLC, www.gradesaver.com

First published in the United States of America by GradeSaver LLC. 2000

GRADESAVER, the GradeSaver logo and the phrase "Getting you the grade since 1999" are registered trademarks of GradeSaver, LLC

ISBN 978-1-60259-103-5

Printed in the United States of America

For other products and additional information please visit

Table of Contents

Table of Contents

Biography of William Golding (1911-1993)

Sir William Gerald Golding was born in 1911 in Saint Columb Minor in Cornwall, England, to Alec Golding, a socialist teacher who supported scientific rationalism, and Mildred Golding (née Curnroe), a supporter of female suffrage. As a child, William Golding was educated at the Marlborough Grammar School, where his father worked, and later at Brasenose College, Oxford. Although educated to be a scientist at the request of his father, the young Golding developed an interest in literature, becoming devoted first to Anglo-Saxon texts and then to poetry, which he wrote avidly. At Oxford he studied natural science for two years and then transfered to a program for English literature and philosophy. Following a short period of time in which he worked in various positions at a settlement house and in small theater companies as both an actor and a writer, Golding became a schoolmaster at Bishop Wordsworth's School in Salisbury. During the Second World War he joined the Royal Navy and was involved in the sinking of the German battleship Bismarck, after which he returned to Bishop Wordsworth's School, where he taught until the early 1960s.

In 1954, Golding published his first novel, Lord of the Flies, which details the adventures of British schoolboys stranded on an island in the Pacific who descend into barbaric behavior. Although at first rejected by twenty-one different publishing houses, Golding's first novel became a surprise success. E.M. Forster declared Lord of the Flies the outstanding novel of its year, while *Time and Tide* called it "not only a first-rate adventure story but a parable of our times." Golding continued to develop similar themes concerning the inherent violence in human nature in his next novel, IThe Inheritors, published the following year. This novel deals with the last days of Neanderthal man. *The Inheritors* posits that the Cro-Magnon "fire-builders" triumphed over Neanderthal man as much by violence and deceit as by any natural superiority. His subsequent works include *Pincher Martin* (1956), the story of a guilt-ridden naval officer who faces an agonizing death, *Free Fall* (1959), and *The Spire* (1964), each of which deals with the depravity of human nature. *The Spire* is an allegory concerning the protagonist's obsessive determination to build a cathedral spire regardless of the consequences.

In addition to his novels and his early collection of poems, Golding published a play entitled *The Brass Butterfly* in 1958 and two collections of essays, *The Hot Gates* (1965) and *A Moving Target* (1982).

Golding's final works include *Darkness Visible* (1979), the story of a boy horribly injured during the London blitz of World War II, and *Rites of Passage* (1980). This novel won the Booker McConnell Prize, the most prestigious award for English literature, and inspired two sequels, *Close Quarters* (1987) and *Fire Down Below* (1989). These three novels portray life aboard a ship during the Napoleonic Wars.

In 1983, Golding received the Nobel Prize for literature for his novels which, according to the Nobel committee, "with the perspicuity of realistic narrative art and the diversity and universality of myth, illuminate the human condition in the world of today." In 1988 he was knighted by Queen Elizabeth II. Sir William died in 1993 in Perranarworthal, Cornwall. At the time of his death he was working on an unfinished manuscript entitled "The Double Tongue," which focused on the fall of Hellenic culture and the rise of Roman civilization. This work was published posthumously in 1995.

About Lord of the Flies

Sir William Golding composed Lord of the Flies shortly after the end of WWII. At the time of the novel's composition, Golding, who had published an anthology of poetry nearly two decades earlier, had been working for a number of years as a teacher and training as a scientist. Golding drew extensively on his scientific background for his first narrative work. The novel's plot, in which a group of English boys stranded on a deserted island struggle to develop their own society, is a social and political thought-experiment using fiction. The story of their attempts at civilization and devolution into savagery and violence puts the relationship between human nature and society under a literary microscope. Golding's allusions to human evolution also reflect his scientific training. The characters discover fire, craft tools, and form political and social systems in a process that recalls theories of the development of early man, a topic of much interest among many peoples including the mid-century Western public. The culmination of the plot in war and murder suggests that Golding's overarching hypothesis about humanity is pessimistic, that is, there are anarchic and brutal instincts in human nature. Ordered democracy or some other regime is necessary to contain these instincts.

As an allegory about human nature and society, Lord of the Flies draws upon Judeo-Christian mythology to elaborate on the novel's sociological and political hypothesis. The title has two meanings, both charged with religious significance. The first is a reference to a line from King Lear, "As flies to wanton boys, are we to gods." The second is a reference to the Hebrew name Ba'alzevuv, or in its Greek form Beelzebub, which translates to "God of the Flies" and is synonymous with Satan. For Golding however, the satanic forces that compel the shocking events on the island come from within the human psyche rather than from an external, supernatural realm as they do in Judeo-Christian mythology. Golding thus employs a religious reference to illustrate a Freudian concept: the Id, the amoral instinct that governs the individual's sense of sheer survival, is by nature evil in its amoral pursuit of its own goals. The Lord of the Flies, that is, the pig's head on a stick, directly challenges the most spiritually motivated character on the island, Simon, who functions as a prophet-martyr for the other boys.

Published in 1954 early in the Cold War, Lord of the Flies is firmly rooted in the sociopolitical concerns of its era. The novel alludes to the Cold War conflict between liberal democracy and totalitarian communism. Ralph represents the liberal tradition, while Jack, before he succumbs to total anarchy, represents the kind of military dictatorship that, for mid-century America and Great Britain, characterized the communist system. It is also notable that Golding sets the novel in what appears to be a future human reality, one that is in crisis after atomic war. Golding's novel capitalizes on public paranoia surrounding the atom bomb which, due to the arms race of the Cold War, was at a high. Golding's negative depiction of Jack, who represents an anti-democratic political system, and his suggestion of the reality of atomic war, present the novel as a gesture of support for the Western position in the

Cold War.

In addition to science, mythology, and the sociopolitical context of the Cold War, Lord of the Flies was heavily influenced by previous works of speculative fiction. In particular, Golding's novel alludes to R. M. Ballantyne's 1857 *The Coral Island*, which tells the story of three boys stranded on a desert island. Golding, who found Ballantyne's interpretation of the situation naive and improbable, likely intended Lord of the Flies to be an indirect critique of *The Coral Island*. Golding preserves the names of two of Ballantyne's characters, Ralph and Jack, to force the two texts into deeper comparison. While the boys of Coral Island spend their time having pleasant adventures, Golding's characters battle hunger, loneliness, and the deadly consequences of political conflict after they are deserted. The pessimistic character of Golding's story reflects the author's emphasis on the necessity of democratic civilization. Critics also have noted the relationship between Lord of the Flies and Joseph Conrad's canonical 1902 Heart of Darkness, which follows a soldier's excursion into marginal African civilizations. Reflecting some biases, Heart of Darkness depicts these parts of Africa as places where social order is absent and anarchy rules, breeding death and disorder; the novel sees the same problem as an issue within the individual human soul. Like Conrad's work, Golding's novel emphasizes the brutal and violent human impulses that arise in the absence of political order.

Lord of the Flies, with its dystopian and speculative characteristics, established Golding as a solid author with an interest in the science-fiction literary genre that was popular in the 1950s. The novel depicts ostensibly realistic characters, but the plot, which follows a small group of humans isolated within an alien landscape, employs or alludes to the conventions of popular science fiction novels of the time. Golding's subsequent works saw him moving even further into the science fiction genre. *The Inheritors*, heavily influenced by H. G. Wells's *Outline of History*, imagines life during the dawn of man and is considered a modern classic of speculative fiction.

Lord of the Flies was not an instant success, selling fewer than 3,000 copies before going out of print in 1955. Shortly thereafter, however, the novel became a bestseller among American and British readers who, as the arms race intensified, likely saw in Golding's wartime dystopia a grim prediction of their own future. By the 1960s the novel was required reading for many high school and college courses, where it has remained to the present day. The enduring popularity of the novel inspired two film adaptations, one by Peter Brook in 1963, and the second by Harry Hook in 1990. Golding's original novel, however, remains the best-known version of the tale. In 2005, *Time Magazine* named the novel one of the 100 best English-language novels since 1923.

A continuing controversy surrounding the political message of the novel and its view of human nature has led some readers to challenge its status as a book suitable for children. The American Library Association thus positioned Lord of the Flies at number 70 on its list of the 100 most challenged books of 1990-2000. Among literary critics of the late twentieth and early twenty-first centuries, however, Lord of the Flies has been revisited less as an allegory of human evil than as a literary expression of Cold War ideology. This historicizing does not do justice to the novel. But in terms of reception history, contemporary critics are right to note that the novel's position at the center of many English curricula across America and Great Britain during the Cold War illustrates how the pedagogy of literature has been used to bolster national identity and ideology.

Character List

Ralph

The protagonist of the story, Ralph is one of the oldest boys on the island. He quickly becomes the group's leader. Golding describes Ralph as tall for his age and handsome, and he presides over the other boys with a natural sense of authority. Although he lacks Piggy's overt intelligence, Ralph is calm and rational, with sound judgment and a strong moral sensibility. But he is susceptible to the same instinctive influences that affect the other boys, as demonstrated by his contribution to Simon's death. Nevertheless, Ralph remains the most civilized character throughout the novel. With his strong commitment to justice and equality, Ralph represents the political tradition of liberal democracy.

Piggy

Although pudgy, awkward, and averse to physical labor because he suffers from asthma, Piggy--who dislikes his nickname--is the intellectual on the island. Though he is an outsider among the other boys, Piggy is eventually accepted by them, albeit grudgingly, when they discover that his glasses can be used to ignite fires. Piggy's intellectual talent endears him to Ralph in particular, who comes to admire and respect him for his clear focus on securing their rescue from the island. Piggy is dedicated to the ideal of civilization and consistently reprimands the other boys for behaving as savages. His continual clashes with the group culminate when Roger murders Piggy by dropping a rock on him, an act that signals the triumph of brute instinct over civilized order. Intellectual, sensitive, and conscientious, Piggy represents culture within the democratic system embodied by Ralph. Piggy's nickname symbolically connects him to the pigs on the island, who quickly become the targets of Jack's and his hunters' bloodlust--an association that foreshadows his murder.

Jack Merridew

The leader of a boys' choir, Jack exemplifies militarism as it borders on authoritarianism. He is cruel and sadistic, preoccupied with hunting and killing pigs. His sadism intensifies throughout the novel, and he eventually turns cruelly on the other boys. Jack feigns an interest in the rules of order established on the island, but only if they allow him to inflict punishment. Jack represents anarchy. His rejection of Ralph's imposed order--and the bloody results of this act--indicate the danger inherent in an anarchic system based only on self-interest.

Simon

The most introspective character in the novel, Simon has a deep affinity with nature and often walks alone in the jungle. While Piggy represents the cultural and Ralph the political and moral facets of civilization, Simon represents the spiritual side of human nature. Like Piggy, Simon is an outcast: the other boys think of him as odd and perhaps insane. It is Simon who finds the beast. When he attempts to tell the group that it is only a dead pilot, the boys, under the impression that he is the beast, murder him in a panic. Golding frequently suggests that Simon is a Christ-figure whose death is a kind of martyrdom. His name, which means "he whom God has heard," indicates the depth of his spirituality and centrality to the novel's Judeo-Christian allegory.

Sam and Eric

The twins are the only boys who remain with Ralph and Piggy to tend to the fire after the others abandon Ralph for Jack's tribe. The others consider the two boys as a single individual, and Golding preserves this perception by combining their individual names into one ("Samneric"). Here one might find suggestions about individualism and human uniqueness.

Roger

One of the hunters and the guard at the castle rock fortress, Roger is Jack's equal in cruelty. Even before the hunters devolve into savagery, Roger is boorish and crude, kicking down sand castles and throwing sand at others. After the other boys lose all idea of civilization, it is Roger who murders Piggy.

Maurice

During the hunters' "Kill the pig" chant, Maurice, who is one of Jack's hunters, pretends to be a pig while the others pretend to slaughter him. When the hunters kill a pig, Jack smears blood on Maurice's face. Maurice represents the mindless masses.

Percival

One of the smallest boys on the island, Percival often attempts to comfort himself by repeating his name and address as a memory of home life. He becomes increasingly hysterical over the course of the novel and requires comforting by the older boys. Percival represents the domestic or familial aspects of civilization; his inability to remember his name and address upon the boys' rescue indicates the erosion of domestic impulse with the overturning of democratic order. Note also that in the literary tradition, Percival was one of the Knights of the Round Table who went in search of the Holy Grail.

The Beast

A dead pilot whom Simon discovers in the forest. The other boys mistake him as a nefarious supernatural omen, "The Beast." They attempt to appease his spirit with The Lord of the Flies.

The Lord of the Flies

The pig's head that Jack impales on a stick as an offering to "The Beast." The boys call the offering "The Lord of the Flies," which in Judeo-Christian mythology refers to Beelzebub, an incarnation of Satan. In the novel, The Lord of the Flies functions totemically; it represents the savagery and amorality of Jack's tribe.

Naval Officer

The naval officer appears in the final scene of the novel, when Ralph encounters him on the beach. He tells Ralph that his ship decided to inspect the island upon seeing a lot of smoke (the outcome of the forest fire that Jack and his tribe had set in the hopes of driving Ralph out of hiding). His naivete about the boys' violent conflict--he believes they are playing a game--underscores the tragedy of the situation on the island. His status as a soldier reminds the reader that the boys' behavior is just a more primitive form of the aggressive and frequently fatal conflicts that characterize adult civilization.

Major Themes

Civilization vs. Savagery

The overarching theme of *Lord of the Flies* is the conflict between the human impulse towards savagery and the rules of civilization which are designed to contain and minimize it. Throughout the novel, the conflict is dramatized by the clash between Ralph and Jack, who respectively represent civilization and savagery. The differing ideologies are expressed by each boy's distinct attitudes towards authority. While Ralph uses his authority to establish rules, protect the good of the group, and enforce the moral and ethical codes of the English society the boys were raised in, Jack is interested in gaining power over the other boys to gratify his most primal impulses. When Jack assumes leadership of his own tribe, he demands the complete subservience of the other boys, who not only serve him but worship him as an idol. Jack's hunger for power suggests that savagery does not resemble anarchy so much as a totalitarian system of exploitation and illicit power.

Golding's emphasis on the negative consequences of savagery can be read as an clear endorsement of civilization. In the early chapters of the novel, he suggests that one of the important functions of civilized society is to provide an outlet for the savage impulses that reside inside each individual. Jack's initial desire to kill pigs to demonstrate his bravery, for example, is channeled into the hunt, which provides needed food for the entire group. As long as he lives within the rules of civilization, Jack is not a threat to the other boys; his impulses are being re-directed into a productive task. Rather, it is when Jack refuses to recognize the validity of society and rejects Ralph's authority that the dangerous aspects of his character truly emerge. Golding suggests that while savagery is perhaps an inescapable fact of human existence, civilization can mitigate its full expression.

The rift between civilization and savagery is also communicated through the novel's major symbols: the conch shell, which is associated with Ralph, and The Lord of the Flies, which is associated with Jack. The conch shell is a powerful marker of democratic order on the island, confirming both Ralph's leadership-determined by election-and the power of assembly among the boys. Yet, as the conflict between Ralph and Jack deepens, the conch shell loses symbolic importance. Jack declares that the conch is meaningless as a symbol of authority and order, and its decline in importance signals the decline of civilization on the island. At the same time, The Lord of the Flies, which is an offering to the mythical "beast" on the island, is increasingly invested with significance as a symbol of the dominance of savagery on the island, and of Jack's authority over the other boys. The Lord of the Flies represents the unification of the boys under Jack's rule as motivated by fear of "outsiders": the beast and those who refuse to accept Jack's authority. The destruction of the conch shell at the scene of Piggy's murder signifies the complete eradication of civilization on the island, while Ralph's demolition of The Lord of the Flies-he intends to use the stick as a spear-signals his own descent into savagery and violence. By the final scene, savagery has completely displaced civilization as the prevailing system on the island.

Individualism vs. Community

One of the key concerns of *Lord of the Flies* is the role of the individual in society. Many of the problems on the island-the extinguishing of the signal fire, the lack of shelters, the mass abandonment of Ralph's camp, and the murder of Piggy-stem from the boys' implicit commitment to a principle of self-interest over the principle of community. That is, the boys would rather fulfill their individual desires than cooperate as a coherent society, which would require that each one act for the good of the group. Accordingly, the principles of individualism and community are symbolized by Jack and Ralph, respectively. Jack wants to "have fun" on the island and satisfy his bloodlust, while Ralph wants to secure the group's rescue, a goal they can achieve only by cooperating. Yet, while Ralph's vision is the most reasonable, it requires work and sacrifice on the part of the other boys, so they quickly shirk their societal duties in favor of fulfilling their individual desires. The shelters do not get built because the boys would rather play; the signal fire is extinguished when Jack's hunters fail to tend to it on schedule.

The boys' self-interestedness culminates, of course, when they decide to join Jack's tribe, a society without communal values whose appeal is that Jack will offer them total freedom. The popularity of his tribe reflects the enormous appeal of a society based on individual freedom and self-interest, but as the reader soon learns, the freedom Jack offers his tribe is illusory. Jack implements punitive and irrational rules and restricts his boys' behavior far more than Ralph did. Golding thus suggests not only that some level of communal system is superior to one based on pure self-interest, but also that pure individual freedom is an impossible value to sustain within a group dynamic, which will always tend towards societal organization. The difficult question, of course, is what individuals are willing to give up to gain the benefits of being in the group.

The Nature of Evil

Is evil innate within the human spirit, or is it an influence from an external source? What role do societal rules and institutions play in the existence of human evil? Does the capacity for evil vary from person to person, or does it depend on the circumstances each individual faces? These questions are at the heart of *Lord of the Flies* which, through detailed depictions of the boys' different responses to their situation, presents a complex articulation of humanity's potential for evil.

It is important to note that Golding's novel rejects supernatural or religious accounts of the origin of human evil. While the boys fear the "beast" as an embodiment of evil similar to the Christian concept of Satan, the novel emphasizes that this interpretation is not only mistaken but also, ironically, the motivation for the boys' increasingly cruel and violent behavior. It is their irrational fear of the beast that informs the boys' paranoia and leads to the fatal schism between Jack and Ralph and their respective followers, and this is what prevents them from recognizing and addressing their responsibility for their own impulses. Rather, as The Lord of the Flies communicates to Simon in the forest glade, the "beast" is an internal force, present in every individual, and is thus incapable of being truly defeated. That the most ethical characters on the island-Simon and Ralph-each come to recognize his own capacity for evil indicates the novel's emphasis on evil's universality among humans.

Even so, the novel is not entirely pessimistic about the human capacity for good. While evil impulses may lurk in every human psyche, the intensity of these impulses-and the ability to control them-appear to vary from individual to individual. Through the different characters, the novel presents a continuum of evil, ranging from Jack and Roger, who are eager to engage in violence and cruelty, to Ralph and Simon, who struggle to contain their brutal instincts. We may note that the characters who struggle most successfully against their evil instincts do so by appealing to ethical or social codes of behavior. For example, Ralph and Piggy demand the return of Piggy's glasses because it is the "right thing to do." Golding suggests that while evil may be present in us all, it can be successfully suppressed by the social norms that are imposed on our behavior from without or by the moral norms we decide are inherently "good," which we can internalize within our wills.

The ambiguous and deeply ironic conclusion of *Lord of the Flies*, however, calls into question society's role in shaping human evil. The naval officer, who repeats Jack's rhetoric of nationalism and militarism, is engaged in a bloody war that is responsible for the boys' aircraft crash on the island and that is mirrored by the civil war among the survivors. In this sense, much of the evil on the island is a result not of the boys' distance from society, but of their internalization of the norms and ideals of that society-norms and ideals that justify and even thrive on war. Are the boys corrupted by the internal pressures of an essentially violent human nature, or have they been corrupted by the environment of war they were raised in? *Lord of the Flies* offers no clear solution to this question, provoking readers to contemplate the complex relationships among society, morality, and human nature.

Man vs. Nature

Lord of the Flies introduces the question of man's ideal relationship with the natural world. Thrust into the completely natural environment of the island, in which no humans exist or have existed, the boys express different attitudes towards nature that reflect their distinct personalities and ideological leanings. The boys' relationships to the natural world generally fall into one of three categories: subjugation of nature, harmony with nature, and subservience to nature. The first category, subjugation of nature, is embodied by Jack, whose first impulse on the island is to track, hunt, and kill pigs. He seeks to impose his human will on the natural world, subjugating it to his desires. Jack's later actions, in particular setting the forest fire, reflect his deepening contempt for nature and demonstrate his militaristic, violent character. The second category, harmony with nature, is embodied by Simon, who finds beauty and peace in the natural environment as exemplified by his initial retreat to the isolated forest glade. For Simon, nature is not man's enemy but is part of the human experience. The third category, subservience to nature, is embodied by Ralph and is the opposite position from Jack's. Unlike Simon, Ralph does not find peaceful harmony with the natural world; like Jack, he understands it as an obstacle to human life on the island. But while Jack responds to this perceived conflict by acting destructively towards animals and plant life, Ralph responds by retreating from the natural world. He does not participate in hunting or in Simon's excursions to the deep wilderness of the forest; rather, he stays on the beach, the most humanized part of the island. As Jack's hunting expresses his violent nature to the other boys and to the reader, Ralph's desire to stay separate from the natural world emphasizes both his reluctance to tempt danger and his affinity for civilization.

Dehumanization of Relationships

In *Lord of the Flies*, one of the effects of the boys' descent into savagery is their increasing inability to recognize each other's humanity. Throughout the novel, Golding uses imagery to imply that the boys are no longer able to distinguish between themselves and the pigs they are hunting and killing for food and sport. In Chapter Four, after the first successful pig hunt, the hunters re-enact the hunt in a ritual dance, using Maurice as a stand-in for the doomed pig. This episode is only a dramatization, but as the boys' collective impulse towards complete savagery grows stronger, the parallels between human and animal intensify. In Chapter Seven, as several of the boys are hunting the beast, they repeat the ritual with Robert as a stand-in for the pig; this time, however, they get consumed by a kind of "frenzy" and come close to actually killing him. In the same scene, Jack jokes that if they do not kill a pig next time, they can kill a littlun in its place. The repeated substitution of boy for pig in the childrens' ritual games, and in their conversation, calls attention to the consequences of their self-gratifying behavior: concerned only with their own base desires, the boys have become unable to see each other as anything more than objects subject to their individual wills. The more pigs the boys kill, the easier it becomes for them to harm and kill each other. Mistreating the pigs facilitates this process of dehumanization.

The early episodes in which boys are substituted for pigs, either verbally or in the hunting dance, also foreshadow the tragic events of the novel's later chapters, notably the murders of Simon and Piggy and the attempt on Ralph's life. Simon, a character who from the outset of the novel is associated with the natural landscape he has an affinity for, is murdered when the other children mistake him for "the beast"-a mythical inhuman creature that serves as an outlet for the children's fear and sadness. Piggy's name links him symbolically to the wild pigs on the island, the immediate target for Jack's violent impulses; from the outset, when the other boys refuse to call him anything but "Piggy," Golding establishes the character as one whose humanity is, in the eyes of the other boys, ambiguous. The murders of Simon and Piggy demonstrate the boys' complete descent into savagery. Both literally (Simon) and symbolically (Piggy), the boys have become indistinguishable from the animals that they stalk and kill.

The Loss of Innocence

At the end of *Lord of the Flies*, Ralph weeps "for the end of innocence," a lament that retroactively makes explicit one of the novel's major concerns, namely, the loss of innocence. When the boys are first deserted on the island, they behave like children, alternating between enjoying their freedom and expressing profound homesickness and fear. By the end of the novel, however, they mirror the warlike behavior of the adults of the Home Counties: they attack, torture, and even murder one another without hesitation or regret. The loss of the boys' innocence on the island runs parallel to, and informs their descent into savagery, and it recalls the Bible's narrative of the Fall of Man from paradise.

Accordingly, the island is coded in the early chapters as a kind of paradise, with idyllic scenery, fresh fruit, and glorious weather. Yet, as in the Biblical Eden, the temptation toward corruption is present: the younger boys fear a "snake-thing." The "snake-thing" is the earliest incarnation of the "beast" that, eventually, will provoke paranoia and division among the group. It also explicitly recalls the snake from the Garden of Eden, the embodiment of Satan who causes Adam and Eve's fall from grace. The boys' increasing belief in the beast indicates their gradual loss of innocence, a descent that culminates in tragedy. We may also note that the landscape of the island itself shifts from an Edenic space to a hellish one, as marked by Ralph's observation of the ocean tide as an impenetrable wall, and by the storm that follows Simon's murder.

The forest glade that Simon retreats to in Chapter Three is another example of how the boys' loss of innocence is registered on the natural landscape of the island. Simon first appreciates the clearing as peaceful and beautiful, but when he returns, he finds The Lord of the Flies impaled at its center, a powerful symbol of how the innocence of childhood has been corrupted by fear and savagery.

Even the most sympathetic boys develop along a character arc that traces a fall from innocence (or, as we might euphemize, a journey into maturity). When Ralph is first introduced, he is acting like a child, splashing in the water, mocking Piggy, and laughing. He tells Piggy that he is certain that his father, a naval commander, will rescue him, a conviction that the reader understands as the wishful thinking of a little boy. Ralph repeats his belief in their rescue throughout the novel, shifting his hope that his own father will discover them to the far more realistic premise that a passing ship will be attracted by the signal fire on the island. By the end of the novel, he has lost hope in the boys' rescue altogether. The progression of

Ralph's character from idealism to pessimistic realism expresses the extent to which life on the island has eradicated his childhood.

The Negative Consequences of War

In addition to its other resonances, *Lord of the Flies* is in part an allegory of the Cold War. Thus, it is deeply concerned with the negative effects of war on individuals and for social relationships. Composed during the Cold War, the novel's action unfolds from a hypothetical atomic war between England and "the Reds," which was a clear word for communists. Golding thus presents the non-violent tensions that were unfolding during the 1950s as culminating into a fatal conflict-a narrative strategy that establishes the novel as a cautionary tale against the dangers of ideological, or "cold," warfare, becoming hot. Moreover, we may understand the conflict among the boys on the island as a reflection of the conflict between the democratic powers of the West and the communist presence throughout China, Eastern Europe, and the Soviet Union. (China's cultural revolution had not yet occurred, but its communist revolution was fresh in Western memory.) Ralph, an embodiment of democracy, clashes tragically with Jack, a character who represents a style of military dictatorship similar to the West's perception of communist leaders such as Joseph Stalin and Mao Zedong. Dressed in a black cape and cap, with flaming red hair, Jack also visually evokes the "Reds" in the fictional world of the novel and the historical U.S.S.R., whose signature colors were red and black. As the tension between the boys comes to a bloody head, the reader sees the dangerous consequences of ideological conflict.

The arrival of the naval officer at the conclusion of the narrative underscores these allegorical points. The officer embodies war and militaristic thinking, and as such, he is symbolically linked to the brutal Jack. The officer is also English and thus linked to the democratic side of the Cold War, which the novel vehemently defends. The implications of the officer's presence are provocative: Golding suggests that even a war waged in the name of civilization can reduce humanity to a state of barbarism. The ultimate scene of the novel, in which the boys weep with grief for the loss of their innocence, implicates contemporary readers in the boys' tragedy. The boys are representatives, however immature and untutored, of the wartime impulses of the period.

Glossary of Terms

"bomb happy"

crazy

"do us"

"kill us"

"give him a fourpenny one"

"hit him in the jaw"

"mucking about"

"wasting time"

"one for his nob"

"a blow to his head"

"round the bend"

crazy

"sod you"

"screw you"

"taken short"

ill with diarrhea

accent

intonation of speech reflecting one's regional or class background; here, Piggy's lower-class pronunciations and slang

acrid

sharp or bitter

altos

those in a choir who sing in the mid-to-high vocal range between soprano and tenor

antiphonal

sung in alternation

barmy

crazy

batty

crazy or odd

bloody

cursed

bollucks

a term of disgust and scorn

bowstave

slightly curved arc

brine

salty water

Coral Island

an 1857 adventure novel by R.M. Ballantyne about a group of boys stranded on a desert island after a shipwreck

cordon

a line or circle of ships or soldiers that guards a certain area

coverts

shelters

cracked

crazy

crackers

crazy; insane

creepers

vines

cutter

a boat carried on larger ships to transport passengers or supplies to shore

Glossary of Terms

dazzle paint

camouflage

derision

contempt or ridicule

diddle

juggle or rattle

diffident

timid or shy

dun

a dull brownish-gray color

embroil

to involve in trouble or conflict

epaulette

a shoulder ornament on military uniforms

essay

to try or attempt

funk

state of panic or fear

gesticulate

to use gestures

Gib., Addis

Gibraltar and Addis Ababa, refueling stations the plane stopped at before crashing

gibber

unintelligible speech

glamor

illusion; spell

ha'porth

contraction of "half-penny's worth," meaning very little

head boy

the honorary title given to a boy who maintains the best personal conduct at his school

Home Counties

the counties around London, England

impervious

not affected by something

inimical

hostile

jolly

very

lamp standard

lamppost

lavatory

toilet

matins

a morning church service with singing

mold

loose, soft soil

myopia

nearsightedness

nuts

expression of contempt; roughly equivalent to "damn"

pax

peace

phosphorescence

a continuing luminescence without heat

pills

testicles

pinch

steal

pinnacles

pointed objects or peaks

plinth

a border of brick or stone running along the base of a wall

polyp

a type of tentacled, tubelike sea creature such as an anemone

precentor

director of a choir

prefect

in English schools, an older student with disciplinary authority over the other students

propitiate

appease

queer

odd or unusual

rating

a man enlisted in the Navy

rebuke

scold or reprimand

Reds

communists

rugger

rugby

scar

plane wreckage left behind after a crash

scurfy

a skin condition that produces a dry, scaly rash

smashing

great

stern sheets

a space at the front (stern) of an open boat

Swallows and Amazons

an adventure novel (1930) by Arthur Ransome about a group of children on vacation, the first in his popular series of adventure books

talisman

an object believed to have magical or protective properties

toilet

the process of grooming oneself

torrid

oppressively hot

Treasure Island

an 1883 novel by Robert Louis Stevenson about a boy's search for buried gold and his encounter with pirates

Trebles

the members of a choir who sing in the highest vocal range

truculent

unapologetically cruel or savage

ululate

howl or wail

wacco

crazy

waxy

enraged

white drill

a coarse kind of cloth (linen or cotton) typically used for uniforms

windy

pompous or boastful

wizard

excellent

Short Summary

During an unnamed time of war, a plane carrying a group of British schoolboys is shot down over the Pacific. The pilot of the plane is killed, but many of the boys survive the crash and find themselves deserted on an uninhabited island, where they are alone without adult supervision. The first two boys introduced are the main protagonists of the story: Ralph is among the oldest of the boys, handsome and confident, while Piggy, as he is derisively called, is a pudgy asthmatic boy with glasses who nevertheless possesses a keen intelligence. Ralph finds a conch shell, and when he blows it the other boys gather together. Among these boys is Jack Merridew, an aggressive boy who marches at the head of his choir. Ralph, whom the other boys choose as chief, leads Jack and another boy, Simon, on an expedition to explore the island. On their expedition they determine that they are, in fact, on a deserted island and decide that they need to find food. The three boys find a pig, which Jack prepares to kill but finally balks before he can actually stab it.

When the boys return from their expedition, Ralph calls a meeting and attempts to set rules of order for the island. Jack agrees with Ralph, for the existence of rules means the existence of punishment for those who break them, but Piggy reprimands Jack for his lack of concern over long-term issues of survival. Ralph proposes that they build a fire on the mountain which could signal their presence to any passing ships. The boys start building the fire, but the younger boys lose interest when the task proves too difficult for them. Piggy proves essential to the process: the boys use his glasses to start the fire. After they start the fire, Piggy loses his temper and criticizes the other boys for not building shelters first. He worries that they still do not know how many boys there are, and he believes that one of them is already missing.

While Jack tries to hunt pigs, Ralph orchestrates the building of shelters for the boys. The smallest boys have not helped at all, while the boys in Jack's choir, whose duty is to hunt for food, have spent the day swimming. Jack tells Ralph that he feels as if he is being hunted himself when he hunts for pigs. When Simon, the only boy who has consistently helped Ralph, leaves presumably to take a bath, Ralph and Jack go to find him at the bathing pool. But Simon instead is walking around the jungle alone. He finds a serene open space with aromatic bushes and flowers.

The boys soon settle into a daily pattern on the island. The youngest of the boys, known generally as the "littluns," spend most of the day searching for fruit to eat. When the boys play, they still obey some sense of decency toward one another, despite the lack of parental authority. Jack continues to hunt, while Piggy, who is accepted as an outsider among the boys, considers building a sundial. A ship passes by the island but does not stop, perhaps because the fire has burned out. Piggy blames Jack for letting the fire die, for he and his hunters have been preoccupied with killing a pig at the expense of their duty, and Jack punches Piggy, breaking one lens of his glasses. Jack and the hunters chant, "Kill the pig. Cut her throat. Bash her in" in celebration of the kill, and they perform a dance in which Maurice pretends to be a pig and the others pretend to attack him.

Ralph becomes concerned by the behavior of Jack and the hunters and begins to appreciate Piggy's maturity. He calls an assembly in which he criticizes the boys for not assisting with the fire or the building of the shelters. He insists that the fire is the most important thing on the island, for it is their one chance for rescue, and declares that the only place where they should have a fire is on the mountaintop. Ralph admits that he is frightened but says that there is no legitimate reason to be afraid. Jack then yells at the littluns for their fear and for not helping with hunting or building shelters. He proclaims that there is no beast on the island, as some of the boys believe, but then a littlun, Phil, tells that he had a nightmare and when he awoke saw something moving among the trees. Simon says that Phil probably saw Simon, for he was walking in the jungle that night. But the littluns begin to worry about the beast, which they conceive as a ghost or a squid. Piggy and Ralph fight once more, and when Ralph attempts to assert the rules of order, Jack asks rhetorically whether anyone cares about the rules. Ralph in turn insists that the rules are all that they have. Jack then decides to lead an expedition to hunt the beast, leaving only Ralph, Piggy and Simon behind. Piggy warns Ralph that if Jack becomes chief, the boys will never be rescued.

That night, during an aerial battle, a pilot parachutes down the island. The pilot dies, possibly on impact. The next morning, as the twins Sam and Eric are adding kindling to the fire, they spot the pilot and mistake him for the beast. They scramble down the mountain and wake up Ralph. Jack calls for a hunt, but Piggy insists that they should stay together, for the beast may not come near them. Jack claims that the conch is now irrelevant. He takes a swing at Ralph when Ralph accuses Jack of not wanting to be rescued. Ralph decides to join the hunters on their expedition to find the beast, despite his wish to rekindle the fire on the mountain. When they reach the other side of the island, Jack expresses his wish to build a fort near the sea.

The hunters, while searching for the beast, find a boar that attacks Jack, but Jack stabs it and it runs away. The hunters go into a frenzy, lapsing into their "kill the pig" chant once again. Ralph realizes that Piggy remains with the littluns back on the other side of the island, and Simon offers to go back and tell Piggy that the other boys will not be back that night. Ralph realizes that Jack hates him and confronts him about that fact. Jack mocks Ralph for not wanting to hunt, claiming that it stems from cowardice, but when the boys see what they believe to be the beast they run away.

Ralph returns to the shelters to find Piggy and tells him that they saw the beast, but Piggy remains skeptical. Ralph dismisses the hunters as boys with sticks, but Jack accuses him of calling his hunters cowards. Jack attempts to assert control over the other boys, calling for Ralph's removal as chief, but when Ralph retains the support of the other boys Jack runs away, crying. Piggy suggests that, if the beast prevents them from getting to the mountaintop, they should build a fire on the beach, and reassures them that they will survive if they behave with common sense. Simon leaves to sit in the open space that he found earlier. Jack claims that he will be the chief of the hunters and that they will go to the castle rock where they plan to build a fort and have a feast. The hunters kill a pig, and Jack smears the blood over Maurice's face. They then cut off the head and leave it on a stake as an offering for the beast. Jack brings several hunters back to the shelters, where he invites the other boys to join his tribe and offers them meat and the opportunity to hunt and have fun. All of the boys, except for Ralph and Piggy, join Jack.

Meanwhile, Simon finds the pig's head that the hunters had left. He dubs it The Lord of the Flies because of the insects that swarm around it. He believes that it speaks to him, telling him how foolish he is and that the other boys think he is insane. The pig's head claims that it is the beast, and it mocks the idea that the beast could be hunted and killed. Simon falls down and loses consciousness. After he regains consciousness and wanders around, he sees the dead pilot that the boys perceived to be the beast and realizes what it actually is. He rushes down the mountain to alert the other boys about what he has found.

Ralph and Piggy, who are playing at the lagoon alone, decide to find the other boys to make sure that nothing unfortunate happens while they are pretending to be hunters. When they find Jack, Ralph and Jack argue over who will be chief. When Piggy claims that he gets to speak because he has the conch, Jack tells him that the conch does not count on his side of the island. The boys panic when Ralph warns them that a storm is coming. As the storm begins, Simon rushes from the forest, telling about the dead body on the mountain. Under the impression that he is the beast, the boys descend on Simon and kill him.

Back on the other side of the island, Ralph and Piggy discuss Simon's death. They both took part in the murder, but they attempt to justify their behavior as motivated by fear and instinct. The only four boys who are not part of Jack's tribe are Ralph and Piggy and the twins, Sam and Eric, who help tend to the fire. At Castle Rock, Jack rules over the boys with the trappings of an idol. He has kept one boy tied up, and he instills fear in the other boys by warning them about the beast and the intruders. When Bill asks Jack how they will start a fire, Jack claims that they will steal the fire from the other boys. Meanwhile, Ralph, Piggy and the twins work on keeping the fire going but find that it is too difficult to do by themselves. They return to the shelters to sleep. During the night, the hunters attack the four boys, who fight them off but suffer considerable injuries. Piggy learns the purpose of the attack: they came to steal his glasses.

After the attack, the four boys decide to go to the castle rock to appeal to Jack as civilized people. They groom themselves to appear presentable and dress themselves in normal schoolboy clothes. When they reach Castle Rock, Ralph summons the other boys with the conch. Jack arrives from hunting and tells Ralph and Piggy to leave them alone. When Jack refuses to listen to Ralph's appeals to justice, Ralph calls the boys painted fools. Jack takes Sam and Eric as prisoners and orders them to be tied up. Piggy asks Jack and his hunters whether it is better to be a pack of painted Indians or sensible like Ralph, but Roger tips a rock over on Piggy, causing him to fall down the mountain to the beach. The impact kills him and, to the delight of Jack, shatters the conch shell. Jack declares himself chief and hurls his spear at Ralph, who runs away.

Ralph hides near Castle Rock, where he can see the other boys, whom he no longer recognizes as civilized English boys but as savages. He crawls to the entrance of Jack's camp, where Sam and Eric are now stationed as guards, and they give him some meat and urge him to leave. While Ralph hides, he realizes that the other boys are rolling rocks down the mountain. Ralph evades the other boys who are hunting for him, then realizes that they are setting the forest on fire in order to smoke him out-and thus will destroy whatever fruit is left on the island.

Running for his life, Ralph finally collapses on the beach, where a naval officer has arrived with his ship. He thinks that the boys have only been playing games, and he scolds them for not behaving in a more organized and responsible manner as is the British custom. As the boys prepare to leave the island for home, Ralph weeps for the death of Piggy and for the end of the boys' innocence.

Summary and Analysis of Chapter One: The Sound of the Shell

On a tropical island, a twelve-year-old boy with fair hair is climbing out of plane wreckage (referred to as "the scar") on a beach and towards a lagoon. He faces another child around his age, a fat boy with glasses. The two, who have not previously met, begin a conversation. The fair-haired boy introduces himself as Ralph, while the heavy boy accidentally reveals his nickname at school: "Piggy." Against the other child's protestations, Ralph insists on calling him Piggy. Through their conversation, it is revealed that the boys have survived a plane crash in the Pacific Ocean, and no adults are present among the survivors. They confirm that both the pilot and "the man with the megaphone"-perhaps some sort of rescue worker-both died in the crash. The boys appear to have been escaping from an atomic war in their country, a place referred to only as the Home Counties (signaling England). When Ralph insists that his father, a Commander in the Navy, will rescue the stranded boys, Piggy reminds him that "they"-perhaps the military, perhaps the adult population-were all killed "by the atom bomb."

Ralph, excited by the idea of living without adult supervision, immediately takes advantage of the freedom on the island. He disrobes and invites Piggy to join him in a swim. Piggy nervously declines, explaining that his asthma prevents him from swimming or running, but eventually-and with much self-consciousness-removes his windbreaker. While Ralph is enjoying the new sights and pleasures of the tropical water, Piggy reveals that his parents are both dead and that he lives with his aunt, who operates a candy store. While Ralph is playing on the shore, Piggy spots a conch shell in the lagoon. He explains to an ignorant Ralph that a conch is valuable, and the two retrieve it from the water. Piggy, who cannot breathe well due to his asthma, instructs Ralph about how to blow into the shell so as to produce a loud whistle. After a few failed attempts, Ralph sounds the shell successfully. The two boys are surprised to see that the sound has attracted other survivors from the crash, among them Sam and Eric, two young identical twins, and abrupt, red-headed Jack Merridew, who is accompanied by a party of boys wearing strange black cloaks and caps, marching in two organized lines. Jack reveals that the group is a boys' choir and that he is the leader.

Once a large group is present, Piggy suggests that everyone state their names. Jack insists on being called Merridew, for Jack is a kid's name, and demands that he be established the leader of the survivors, for he is the head boy of his choir. The group decides to settle the question of leadership by vote. While Jack has natural leadership qualities and Piggy rational intelligence, Ralph has a calm personality that invites the others' trust, so he is elected chief. Once appointed, however, Ralph concedes that Jack may still lead his choir, who will become hunters. He further insists that the group stay assembled near the lagoon while three of the boys explore the territory to determine whether or not it is an island. For this task, Ralph chooses himself, a mild-tempered boy named Simon, and, at his own insistence, Jack. When Piggy requests to join the explorers, Jack dismisses the idea, humiliating Piggy, who is still ashamed that Ralph revealed his hated nickname.

Ralph, Simon and Jack search the island, climbing up the mountain to survey it. On the way up, they push down the mountain a large rock that blocks their way. When they finally reach the top, they determine that they are indeed on an island. The island is described as "boat-shaped," bordered by rocks and containing both lagoon and forest areas. Ralph, looking at the landscape, says assertively, "this belongs to us." The three decide that they need food to eat, and continue to explore the island, this time in search of food.

The boys descend the mountain into brush area, where they consider and then decide against eating some foliage they call "candle-buds." Shortly thereafter, they discover a piglet caught in a curtain of creepers. Jack draws his knife but pauses before he has a chance to stab the pig, which frees itself and runs away. Jack insists that he was merely looking for the right spot on the pig on which to stab it, but his white face suggests that he is unaccustomed to such violence. But he vows that next time, he will show no mercy toward his prey.

Analysis

The opening chapter of Lord of the Flies establishes the novel as a political allegory. As a whole, the novel explores the need for political organization and dramatizes the clash in human nature between instinctual and learned behavior. In Chapter One, Golding depicts the deserted island as a place where the abandoned boys have a choice between returning to a pre-civilized state of humanity and re-imposing social order upon the group. Thus, the situation tests a Hobbesian hypothesis by throwing the children almost fully into a state of nature. The first chapter of the novel confirms that the boys have no society, no rules, and no concerns beyond personal survival. All they have is a set of histories. The narrative thrust of the novel traces how the boys develop their own miniature society and the difficulties that inevitably arise from this development. Chapter One foreshadows these events by depicting the boys as alternately frightened, ignorant, and exhilarated in the face of their newfound freedom.

Accordingly, Chapter One immediately establishes the tension between the impulse towards savagery and the need for civilization that exists within the human spirit. Freed from adult authority and the mores of society, Ralph plays in the beach naked, a practice that at the time of Golding's writing was commonly associated with pre-industrial cultures believed to be "uncivilized" or "savage." Yet if Ralph's nudity is an uncivilized practice, it is also a reference to another popular conception of pre-civilized life, that of the Garden of Eden. Ralph does not panic over the children's abandonment on the island, but he approaches it as a paradise in which he can play happily. The reader, aware of the outcome of the Biblical Eden, should treat the boys' "paradise" with similar skepticism. Like Eden, the island paradise will collapse; the questions are how and why.

Characterization emphasizes the tension Golding establishes between anarchy and political organization. The first sign of disturbance on the seemingly tranquil island is the appearance of Jack and his choir. Golding describes Jack and his compatriots as militaristic and aggressive, with Jack's bold manner and the choir marching in step. They are the first concrete example of civilization on the island, with a decidedly negative feel. Jack seems a physical manifestation of evil; with his dark cloak and wild red hair, his appearance is ominous, even Satanic. Accordingly, Jack is militaristic and authoritarian. He gives orders to his choir as if they were troops, allowing room for neither discussion nor dissent. Significantly, the role that he first chooses for his choir is that of hunters-he selects that task which is most violent and most related to military values. Yet, as his inability to kill the pig demonstrates, Jack is not yet accustomed to violence. Golding indicates that Jack must prepare himself to commit a violent act, for he is still constrained by his own youthful cowardice or by societal rules that oppose violent behavior. While his authoritarian attitude indicates a predisposition to violence, Jack must shed the lessons of society and conscience before he can kill.

In both temperament and physical appearance, Ralph is the antithesis of Jack. Golding idealizes Ralph from the beginning, lavishing praise on his physical beauty. In the island sun he immediately achieves a golden hue, a physical manifestation of his winning charisma. Ralph's value is not intellectual; importantly, he behaves somewhat childishly in his first encounter with Piggy. Still, Golding suggests that Ralph has a gravity and maturity beyond his years. He is a natural leader, a quality that the other boys immediately recognize when they vote him leader. The vote for chief establishes a conflict between the different values espoused by Jack and Ralph. Jack assumes that he should assume the role automatically, while Ralph, who is reluctant to accept leadership, achieves it by vote. Ralph therefore comes to represent a democratic ethos.

In contrast to the violent Jack and charismatic Ralph, Piggy is immediately established as the intellectual of the group. Although he is physically inept, clumsy, and asthmatic, he has a rational mind and the best grasp of their situation. It is his knowledge of the conch shell that allows Ralph to summon the rest of the boys together and he who shows the most concern for some sort of established order in meetings and in day-to-day life. He has a particular interest in names, immediately asking Ralph for his and wishing that Ralph would reciprocate the question, as well as insisting that a list of names be taken when the boys assemble. This emphasis on naming is one of the first indications of the imposition of an ordered society on the island (it also recalls the naming of the animals in Genesis). For Piggy, names not only facilitate organization and communication but also mark one's position within a social hierarchy. It is significant that Piggy is forced by the others to keep his despised nickname from home, which re-inscribes his inferior social status from the Home Counties in the new dynamic of the island. We may also note that Piggy's name symbolically connects him to the pigs on the island, which in subsequent chapters become the targets of many of the boys' unrestrained violent impulses. As the boys turn their rage against the pigs, Golding foreshadows Piggy's own murder at the close of the novel.

The reinforcement of Piggy's nickname, which clearly humiliates him, also indicates that the boys have imported to the island the cruelty of human social life. Ralph's mockery of Piggy is the first instance of inequality on the island, and it foreshadows the gross inequities and injustices to come. We may also note here Piggy's background (as an orphan who lives with an aunt) and his poor diction ("can't catch me breath," "what's yer name?")-details that indicate that, unlike Ralph and Jack, Piggy is a child from a working-class background. His immediate ostracizing on the island suggests another way in which the social hierarchies of the boys' home lives are reproduced in island life. Golding suggests that Piggy's marginalization is due not only to his unfortunate appearance and poor health but also because he is of a lower class status than the other boys, who have brought with them to the island the class prejudices of the Home Counties.

It is also significant here that Golding emphasizes the establishment of property and subtly critiques the concept of ownership by discovery. Ralph gains status from his possession of the conch shell, which gives him the authority to speak when the boys come together. Also, when he surveys the island from the summit of the mountain he states that it "belongs" to them, almost as an act of colonization or conquering. The invocation of colonial rhetoric suggests the struggles to come over ownership of the key resources on the island (such as the conch and Piggy's glasses) and over the power to rule one another.

The novel's first chapter establishes another theme that recurs throughout the novel: the corruption of innocence. Golding emphasizes the childish nature of the boys from the outset of the narrative, and he suggests that many of the struggles that mark their time on the island have less to do with either the natural brutality of the human spirit or the corruption of political society than with the boys' young age and incapacity for responsibility. Ralph's first reaction to the abandonment is to play in the water, and Jack's impulse to "kill" falls flat when he is confronted with an opportunity to do so. The chatter of the younger boys-who fear a "beastie" and a "snake thing," as well as Piggy's constant mention of his "auntie" at home who gave him candy, are narrative details that underscore the boys' youth and their essential innocence. As the brutality and violence among the boys increase in later chapters, Golding suggests that childhood is a neutral, formative state in which children can either be guided towards morality or corrupted by savagery when they are unguided by conscience or society. The emphasis on the boys' childishness in Chapter One establishes important questions that the subsequent action seeks to answer: is human nature essentially good, bad, or neutral, and how do early childhood experiences inform individual character?

Summary and Analysis of Chapter Two: Fire on the Mountain

Back with the group the same evening, Ralph blows the conch shell to call another meeting. The effects of abandonment are visible in the boys' attire: the sunburned children have put on clothing once more, while the choir is more disheveled, having abandoned their cloaks. When the group of boys give Ralph full attention, Ralph suffers a brief lapse in confidence and is unsure whether to stand or sit while conducting a meeting. He looks to Piggy for affirmation of his authority. Ralph announces to the boys the results of the morning's explorations. He explains that they are on an uninhabited island. At this point, Jack interjects and insists that they need an army to hunt the pigs. Ralph, Jack, and Piggy excitedly describe to the others their encounter with the piglet, Jack insisting defensively that it "got away" before he had the chance to stab and kill it, and vowing again to kill it "next time." To demonstrate his sincerity, Jack dramatically plunges his knife into a tree trunk, and the children, made uneasy by Jack's boldness, fall into silence.

Recognizing that the meeting has devolved into disorder, Ralph announces that they will have to establish rules, not only in meetings, but also to organize day-to-day life. He states that, in meetings, the boys will have to raise their hands, like in school, so as to ensure that they speak one at a time. The boy whose turn it is to speak will receive the conch shell, which he will hold while talking, and then will pass it along to the next speaker. Jack interrupts to approve of the imposition of rules, and he begins excitedly explaining the punishment that will result from breaking them. Piggy, grabbing the conch from Ralph, reprimands Jack for "hindering Ralph." He says that the most important thing is that nobody knows where they are and that they may be there a long time. The boys fall into an anxious silence.

Ralph, taking the conch again from Piggy, reassures the other boys, explaining that the island is theirs-and until the grown-ups come they will have fun. He says that it will be like a novel, and the others, excited once more, begin shouting the names of their favorite island adventure novels: Treasure Island, *Swallows and Amazons*, and *The Coral Island*. Ralph quiets the assembly by waving the conch. A small six-year-old boy whose face is half-covered by a red birthmark stands hesitantly to request the conch. He appears as if he is about to cry; once he has possession of the conch, he asks Ralph what the group will do about a snake-thing, which he describes as a "beastie" that appeared to him in the forest. Ralph assures the group that such animals only live in large countries, like those in Africa, so the boy must have dreamt the beastie in the aftermath of the crash. The boys seem largely reassured, though Ralph notices some signs of doubt on the faces of the younger children.

Ralph tells the boys that their goal while stranded shall be twofold: one, they should try to ensure their rescue, and two, they should try to have fun. He assures them that, as his Naval Commander father told him, there are no unknown islands on the planet, and thus they will be rescued. The others break into spontaneous applause at Ralph's confidence in their rescue. He then explains to the group the details of his rescue plan. Ralph suggests that they build a fire on the top of the mountain, for the smoke will signal their presence to passing ships. Jack summons the boys to come build a fire on the mountaintop, and they immediately follow, leaving Piggy and Ralph behind to discuss the outcome of the meeting.

Piggy expresses disgust at the childish behavior of the boys as Ralph catches up to the group and helps them carry piles of wood to the mountaintop. Eventually, the task proves too difficult for some of the smaller boys, who lose interest and search for fruit to eat. When they have gathered enough wood, Ralph and Jack wonder how to start a fire. Piggy arrives, and Jack suggests that they use his glasses. Jack snatches the glasses from Piggy, who can barely see without them. A boy named Maurice suggests that they use green branches to ignite the fire. After a few attempts, the glasses concentrate the rays of the sun and start a fire. Though the boys are mesmerized by the fire, it soon burns out. Piggy, disheartened by the waste of their only firewood, chastises Jack, and the two argue bitterly.

Ralph grabs the conch from Piggy and again reminds the group of the importance of rules. Jack agrees, explaining that they are not savages, they are English, and the English are the best at everything, so they must follow the right rules. Ralph concedes they might never be saved, and Piggy claims that he has been saying that, but nobody has listened. They get the fire going once more. While Piggy has the conch, he loses his temper again, telling the other boys they should have listened to his earlier orders to build shelters first while a fire is of secondary importance. Piggy worries that they still do not know exactly how many boys there are, and he mentions the snakes. Suddenly, one of the trees catches on fire, and one of the boys screams about snakes. Piggy thinks that one of the boys is missing.

Analysis

In the novel's second chapter, Golding uses the progress of the boys on the island as a metaphor for early human development. The boys' first achievement on the island is to build a fire, which like the conch shell brings the entire group of boys together in awe and wonder. According to Piggy, the next step should be for the boys to build some sort of shelter, again a mirror of the historical development of early human society. The "government" established by Ralph also develops during this chapter. Golding uses these developments to signal that the island is becoming a society with rules that mirror Western democratic culture. The conch shell, which authorizes its holder to speak and is available to all, is a particular symbol of the ideal of democratic freedom and equality. But, since Ralph decides who gets possession of the conch, the freedoms of the island are decided by authority. Though Ralph is a benevolent leader, the implication here is that democracy still depends on its leaders for justice.

Also like a democratic system, the makeshift government on the island sparks debate and dissent. Jack and Piggy have differing perspectives on what particular end

Ralph's rules will serve. Ralph takes a rational perspective based on ideas of justice: the rules will allow the boys to live fairly with one another, a belief that fits well with his democratic sensibility. Jack relishes the idea of rules as a means for control and for punishment, a reflection of his dictatorial ethos and tendency toward violence. Piggy, as the most intelligent of the three central characters, views the rules as useful tools for survival. He views all aspects of the boys' behavior on the island in terms of whether they will contribute to their eventual rescue.

Golding continues to present Ralph as a calming, authoritative presence among the boys. When fear sets in among some of the younger boys, only Ralph has the presence to restore order and hope. Despite Piggy's clear thinking and appraisal of their situation, his contentious manner and rude dismissal of the younger boys unfortunately causes his ideas to be dismissed. Even more importantly, he is a cynic who can do nothing to comfort the others, instead instilling in them a sense of fatalism. Piggy, whose pessimism and sadness make him a likely martyr, is established in this chapter as a prophet whose words are not heeded until it is too late. Golding uses Piggy's advice as foreshadowing: failure to heed Piggy, however absurd he may sound, leads to dire consequences. Chapter Two contains the first example of Piggy's prophecy: after the trip to the mountain, one of the boys seems to be missing. The implication is that if the others had heeded Piggy's advice and allowed him to keep track of the number of boys and their names, there would be no confusion over whether one is missing.

Despite the boys' dislike for Piggy, they appear to recognize that he is an important presence on the island. His glasses enable them to start a fire on the mountain. In particular, Piggy is useful for Jack, who remains more interested in hunting and causing pain and disorder than in contributing or constructing anything of use. It is significant that the development he is most supportive of is building a fire, which is by nature destructive even though it can be used for good. In this chapter, Golding also establishes Jack as a boy who tends to dominate. Jack's statement about the English being the "best at everything" also suggests his nationalistic impulses. Jack adheres to the colonial English position that depended on the perceived superiority of the British to justify the colonization and forced development of other peoples, foreshadowing his brutal behavior in subsequent chapters. His statement that they are "not savages" will, by the end of the novel, appear deeply ironic as Jack and his tribe devolve into unthinkable depths of brutality and self-destruction.

The boys' childishness is again highlighted as the boys face the challenge of meeting their basic needs for survival. The immediate dangers that the boys face are few, for on the island there is fruit, plus the pigs, to eat, yet as children they are overcome with irrational and diffuse terror. Golding suggests that their own sense of fear is the greatest danger to these boys. It is fear over a snake that causes the younger boys to panic and to exaggerate the dangers on the island, causing disorder and commotion. Both Jack and Piggy contribute to this sense of dread. Jack does so through his aggressive stance, which contains the implicit notion that they are in danger and must defend themselves from some unknown force. Piggy does so through his constant fatalism. It is here that Ralph best demonstrates his superiority for leadership, displaying the most calm of any of the characters and encouraging the others to be confident in their rescue. Ralph is established here not only as a political leader but also as a parental figure whose job is to reassure the scared boys and protect them from their own fears and doubts.

As the narrative moves closer to dramatic conflict and tragedy, Golding distinguishes Lord of the Flies from the romantic adventure stories that were popular among boys of the mid-twentieth century. In the second meeting, Ralph encourages the boys to have fun on the island and to think of the experience as one that would happen "in a novel." Immediately, the boys begin shouting out the names of their favorite island adventures, including *The Coral Island*. *The Coral Island* (1857), written by R.M. Ballantyne, was a popular nineteenth-century novel that followed the happy adventures of three unsupervised boys on a tropical island. Golding, who found the narrative of *The Coral Island* naive and unlikely, wrote Lord of the Flies partly as a response to this novel. The mention of these idealized island narratives at the outset of Golding's dystopian tale is thus ironic because the events to follow are nothing like the entertaining experiences of the boys on *The Coral Island*. Through the explicit comparison, the reader is encouraged to recognize Golding's work as a critical commentary on popular adventure fiction on the basis of its optimistic unreality.

Also in Chapter Two, Golding introduces more symbols that will recur throughout the novel and which highlight important developments in the dramatic action. The fire that the boys build signifies the group's hope for their rescue and return to the Home Counties. A powerful symbol of human civilization, the fire is a marker of the imposition of human industry on wild, untamed nature; the boys' inability to maintain the fire indicates the waning possibility of both rescue and maintaining civilized order on the island. We may also note the introduction in this chapter of the "beastie," or as it is later known, the "beast." The idea of the beast is first mentioned by one of the younger boys though it is dismissed by most of the older children. As Ralph reassures them, he sees a glimmer of doubt in many of their expressions, an observation that mirrors the group's eventual acceptance of the beast as a legitimate if improbable reality. The beast becomes an important motif that establishes the power and danger of group-think among the boys.

Summary and Analysis of Chapter Three: Huts on the Beach

Jack scans the oppressively silent forest, looking for pigs to hunt. A bird startles him as he progresses along the trail. He examines the texture of vines ("creepers") to determine whether or not pigs have run through that section of the brush. Finally, Jack spots a path cleared by pigs (a "pig run") and hears the pattering of hooves. He raises his spear and hurls it at a group of pigs, driving them away and thus feeling a profound sense of impotence and frustration. The length of Jack's hair, the mass of freckles on his tanned back, and the tattered condition of his shorts indicate that weeks have passed since the boys were abandoned on the island. Jack appears to have taken up his role as group hunter with zeal, and he at least has become talented at tracking pigs in the dense brush.

Having frightened off the pigs without a kill, Jack abandons the hunt and returns to a clearing in the forest, where the boys are constructing crude shelters out of tree trunks and palm leaves. He comes upon Ralph, who is working on a shelter facing the lagoon. Jack asks Ralph for water, who directs him to a tree where coconut shells full of water are arranged. After Jack quenches his thirst, Ralph complains to Jack that the boys are not working hard to build the shelters. The little ones-referred to now as "littluns," are hopeless, spending most of their time bathing or eating. Jack reminds Ralph that he and his hunters are working hard to ensure that the group is always fed.

Jack then tells Ralph that as chief he should just order them to work harder. Ralph admits that even if he called a meeting, the group would agree to five minutes of work and then "wander off to go hunting." Recognizing this as a slight against himself and his hunters, Jack blushes, and he explains that the group is hungry. Ralph points out that Jack's group has yet to bring any meat back from the forest-the hunters would rather swim than hunt. Jack explains that he has little control over his hunters, but he has been working hard himself to "kill." A "madness" flashes in his eyes when he vows to kill a pig, but Ralph again reminds him that he has not yet captured any prey.

The two argue about Jack's contributions to the society on the island, Jack vowing to kill prey and Ralph insisting that they need shelters more than anything. Ralph mentions that the other boys, especially the littluns, are frightened and scream in the middle of the night. The two are interrupted by Simon, who reminds Ralph and Jack about the littluns' fear of the "beastie." The three reminisce about their first day on the island, when they explored the unknown territory together. They laugh that the littluns are "crackers." Jack says that when he is hunting he often feels as if he is being hunted, but he admits that this is irrational. Nevertheless, he says, he knows "how they feel."

Ralph ignores this confession and reminds Jack to remember the fire when he is out hunting. Ralph and Jack make their way to the mountain to inspect the fire, leaving Simon behind. The two speculate as to whether or not the fire is strong enough to signal a passing ship, but Jack is distracted again by thoughts of killing a pig. Ralph, indignant at Jack's preoccupation with hunting, accuses him again of not contributing to the project of building shelters. Not wanting to start a fruitless argument, however, Ralph points out the other boys near the bathing pool and explains that Simon has worked as hard as he has at building shelters. The two make their way back to the huts in search of Simon, but he is nowhere to be found. Ralph, disappointed and confused, pronounces Simon "queer" and "funny." The two boys decide to go swimming together in the island bathing pool and soon find that the tension between them has dissolved.

In the forest, Simon is wandering alone. Simon followed Jack and Ralph halfway up the beach toward the mountain, then turned into the forest with a sense of purpose. He is a tall, skinny boy with a coarse mop of black hair, brilliant eyes, and bare feet. He walks through the acres of fruit trees and finds fruit that the smallest boys cannot reach. He gives the boys fruit, then proceeds along the path into the jungle. He finds an open space and looks to see whether he is alone. This open space contains great aromatic bushes, a bowl of heat and light. Simon eagerly takes in the complex sensations of the forest, and he stays peacefully enclosed in a "cabin" of leaves until long after day has faded into night.

Analysis

The main focus of this short chapter is the developing conflict between Ralph and Jack. The two engage in a verbal argument that indicates that each character is clinging dogmatically to his own perspective. What is more, they represent opposing ideologies. While Ralph is dedicated to building shelters for the group, Jack is determined to become a successful hunter and establish himself as a lone hero among the group. Ralph's orientation is towards the group, while Jack is concerned with his own glory, which hinges again on militaristic values. Jack seeks to dominate and conquer nature through hunting and killing pigs, a goal that foreshadows the intensification of his violent impulses throughout the novel and further identifies him as a symbol for totalitarian, as opposed to democratic, political organization.

The chapter's beginning follows Jack on a solitary hunt through the forest, which underscores Jack's importance to the novel and explains his preoccupation with hunting. For Jack, hunting is not an instinctive talent but a skill that he continues to develop as the story unfolds. His motives for hunting are disturbing. He hunts not for the ostensible purpose of gaining food to eat but for his personal enjoyment. Golding indicates that there is something tremendously dangerous in Jack's obsession; his expression is one of "madness" when he speaks about his desire to kill. At this point in the story Jack is not sufficiently prepared to kill, but he is approaching the point at which he can inflict mortal violence upon another, whether a pig or a person. Ralph cannily realizes this trait when he reminds Jack that the most important thing that the boys must do is to build a shelter. He implicitly tells Jack that his obsession with hunting does not help the boys' chances of survival.

Golding also elaborates on Ralph's character, which is presented as sympathetic, rational, and focused on the group's welfare. Still, he is not a perfect leader. He expresses regret and frustration that he cannot control the behavior of the other boys. The major burden that Ralph faces is that he must deal with young children unprepared to care for themselves or fulfill responsibility. As he explains, Ralph cannot simply give them orders and expect them to be completed, as Jack automatically assumes he can. Ralph alerts the reader to one of the major obstacles that the boys must overcome: they must behave beyond their years in order to survive and flourish long enough to be saved.

We may also note in Chapter Three the changes in the characters' appearances and in the language they use. There is a significant gap of time between this chapter and the last, and the boys have grown farther from the conventions and values of the Home Counties. Jack hunts in the forest half-naked, and many of the boys wear "tattered shorts" or have bare feet, details that indicate that they have abandoned the ways of home in favor of comfort and ease. Moreover, the younger boys, referred to as "little ones" in the previous chapters, are now called "littluns," and Sam and Eric, the twins, have become "Samneric," a compound that suggests that, in the eyes of the group, the two characters are considered one. In the absence of external authority, the boys have developed their own dress code and are beginning to establish their own language. It is becoming an independent culture. Golding reinforces the latter detail by reproducing the boys' own invented words-"littluns" and "Samneric"-in his own third-person prose. The implication is that the boys' civilization is less a mirror of their upbringing than it is a reflection of the unique concerns and dynamics of life on the island.

Chapter Three provides the reader with more insight into Simon's character. Simon was introduced in Chapter One but is not important until he interrupts Ralph's and Jack's argument. Described as barefoot, long-haired, and alternately "queer" and "funny," Simon is revealed as socially outcast from the other boys. Yet, unlike Piggy, Simon seems content with his difference and even cultivates it. When he, Ralph, and Jack decide to go look at the signal fire, Simon abruptly abandons the mission without word in order to wander off into the forest with a sense of "purpose." Ignoring the usual rules of social interaction, which would require him to tell the others of his plans out of politeness, Simon distinguishes himself as ruled not by society but by an intense and even spiritual inner force. His long hair and bare feet connect him not only to nature but to the stereotypical wandering prophet or even Jesus Christ, a link that the novel will enforce further with his murder.

Simon's experience in the jungle, which we read in detail, emphasizes his spiritual and peaceful character. The open space that he settles into in the jungle is an indication that, for Simon, the island is indeed Edenic. Unlike Ralph, who seeks to protect the group from nature, and Jack, who seeks to conquer and control it, Simon views the natural landscape as a place of beauty and tranquility. His excursion shows that he is the one character having an affinity with the natural world. There are strong religious overtones in Golding's description of the area that Simon finds. With its candle-buds, serene stillness, and leafy walls, it recalls a place of worship.

While the dialogue in Chapter Three highlights the ideological contrast between Jack and Ralph, on a structural level, Golding also forces Jack and Simon into comparison. The chapter begins and concludes in the forest, linking both characters to the area (in contrast to Ralph, who is associated with the beach and mountain areas that he has marked with symbols of civilization-the fire and shelters). Jack and Simon are both anti-civilizing characters, attracted to the wild, untamed environment of nature, which they prefer to experience in solitude and silence. Nevertheless, their experiences of the forest are markedly distinct. While Jack disturbs and disrupts his surroundings, causing both birds and pigs to flee, Simon feels in complete harmony with the natural world. He submerges himself in the rhythms of the forest not to disturb it, but to appreciate its unique sounds, scents, and images. Jack and Simon thus represent two different human approaches to the natural world: the desire to subjugate nature and the desire to coexist in harmony with it. Within this schema, Ralph and Piggy represent a third position, that which seeks to retreat from but make use of nature with a distant but tangible respect.

Summary and Analysis of Chapter Four: Painted Faces and Long Hair

The boys become accustomed to the pattern of their days on the island although it is impossible to adjust to the new rhythms of tropical life, which include the strange point at midday when the sea rises and appears to contain flickering images. Piggy discounts the midday illusions as mere mirages. While mornings are cool and comfortable, the afternoon sun is oppressively hot and bright, which incites fatigue among many of the boys. The northern European tradition of work, play, and food right through the day is not forgotten, making the transition difficult.

As the boys settle into life on the island, factions develop. The smaller boys are now known by the generic title of "littluns," including Percival, the smallest boy on the island, who had previously stayed in a small shelter for two days and had only recently emerged, red-eyed and miserable. The littluns spend most of the day searching for fruit to eat, and since they choose it indiscriminately they suffer from chronic diarrhea. They cry for their mothers less often than expected, and they spend time with the older boys only during Ralph's assemblies. The littluns occupy themselves by building castles in the sand, complex structures whose fine details are only noticeable from close range. The littluns remain collectively troubled by nightmares and visions of the "beastie" described at the first meeting. They fear that the creature hunts the boys after nightfall.

Two older boys, Roger and Maurice, come out of the forest for a swim and, expressing their superiority over the littluns, begin to kick down the sand castles on the shore. Maurice, remembering that his mother chastised him for such behavior, feels guilty when he gets sand in Percival's eye. While this conflict unfolds, Henry-a littlun who is related to the boy who disappeared-is preoccupied by some small creatures on the beach, which he finds fascinating. Roger picks up a stone to throw at Henry but deliberately misses him when he throws it, recalling the taboos of earlier life.

Jack thinks about why he is still unsuccessful as a hunter. He believes that the animals see him, so he wants to find some way to camouflage himself. Jack rubs his face with charcoal and laughs with a bloodthirsty snarl when he sees his reflection in a pool of water. From behind the mask, Jack appears liberated from shame and self-consciousness.

Piggy thinks about making a sundial so that they can tell time and better organize their days, but Ralph dismisses the idea. The idea that Piggy is an outsider is tacitly accepted. Ralph believes that he sees smoke along the horizon coming from a ship, but there is not enough smoke from the mountain to signal it. Ralph starts to run to the up the mountain, but he is too late. Their signal fire is dead. Ralph screams for the ship to come back, but it passes without seeing them. Frustrated and sad, Ralph places the blame on the hunters, whose job it was to tend the fire.

From the forest, Jack and the hunters return covered in paint and humming a bizarre war chant. Ralph sees that the hunt has finally been successful: they are carrying a dead pig on a stick. Nevertheless, Ralph admonishes them for letting the fire go out. Jack, however, is overjoyed by the kill and ignores Ralph. Piggy begins to cry at their lost opportunity, and he also blames Jack. The two argue, and finally Jack punches Piggy in the stomach. Piggy's glasses fly off, and one of the lenses breaks on the rocks. Jack eventually does apologize about the fire, but Ralph resents Jack's misbehavior. Jack considers not letting Piggy have any meat, but he orders everyone to eat. Maurice pretends to be a pig, and the hunters circle around him, dancing and singing, "Kill the pig. Cut her throat. Bash her in." Ralph vows to call an assembly.

Analysis

Golding begins the chapter by describing a sense of order among the boys on the island, and he concludes it by describing the order's disintegration. Even the smallest boys appear to have accepted their fate on the island, and they have developed strategies, such as the building of sand castles, to minimize and contain their anguish. The key to the initial tranquility on the island is the maintenance of customs from the society in which the boys were raised. Yet, as the chapter's opening passages imply, these customs are threatened by the natural forces at work on the island. The regular schedule of work, play time, and meal time is impossible in the volatile tropical atmosphere. That the boys do not know whether the movement of the mid-afternoon sea is real or a "mirage" indicates how ill-adjusted to the island they still are.

We begin to focus on the boys'-particularly Jack's-transgression of the ordered rules of their invented society. Golding highlights how life on the island has begun to mirror human society, with the boys organizing themselves into cliques according to age and placing these cliques in a social hierarchy. The littluns have their own routines and separate themselves from the older boys. The intricate sandcastles the littluns build on the shore represent their continued respect for-even idealization of-human civilization, and their continuing presence at Ralph's meetings signals the littluns' investment in ordered island life, even though they do not contribute directly to the group's survival. Golding employs the littluns as symbols for the weak members of society that a successful democracy strives to protect.

The episode with Roger and Maurice kicking down the sandcastles thus signals the disintegration of ordered life on the island, and it foreshadows the end of Ralph's democratic plans. The sandcastles are a miniature civilization on the shore. By destroying the sandcastles, Roger and Maurice not only express an abusive power over the younger boys but indicate their increasing disrespect for civilized order and human institutions. Still, Golding suggests, they have not yet devolved into complete savagery. Maurice, remembering his mother's discipline, feels guilty about kicking sand into Percival's eye, and Roger refrains from throwing a stone at Henry. The implication is that the influences of human society are difficult to erase from the human psyche; they remain internalized even in the absence of rules, and conscience retains its hold. Whatever lessons the boys' past had instilled in them prove critical to maintaining some semblance of peace on the island. Despite the stirrings of anarchy, the boys obey notions of appropriate behavior without any real external authority to determine what they can and cannot do. It is only when the boys completely transgress these civilized norms that they suffer.

Jack is the first to seriously overstep the boundaries of civilized society. His attempts to become a successful hunter are in effect attempts to succumb entirely to his animalistic nature. His painted face, reminiscent of some less developed societies, supposedly makes him indistinguishable from the animals of the forest. When Jack finally does kill a pig, as he has intended to do since the beginning of the novel, he fulfills a violent blood-lust that, until then, had remained frustrated. The other hunters share this quality; when they dance and sing about killing the pig, they show that they have succumbed to the thrill of violence. They relish the slaughter, an enjoyment that transcends pride and signifies pure lust. As they cheer on the means by which they mutilate the pig, their painted skin, chanting, and frenzy suggest they have developed their own sub-society, one based on rituals and an almost spiritual worship of blood, violence, and slaughter.

Maurice's impression of the pig during the dance calls attention to the increasingly indistinct line between violence against animals on the island and violence among the boys. Significantly, this chapter contains the first instance of explicit aggression between two boys. Jack, now accustomed to harming others with his recent kill, punches Piggy, who, as Golding reminds us, remains an outsider. The chapter further sets up Piggy as a martyr. He has the most grounded concerns of all the boys, and he offers the reasonable proposal that they construct a sundial, but he is also loathed by the others. Only Ralph, the most mature and grounded of the characters, sympathizes with Piggy and agrees with him that Jack made an egregious error by letting the fire go out. Piggy stands apart from the other boys, for he retains the goal of living in an increasingly civilized society. His hair does not even seem to grow, helping him retain the appearance of a normal English schoolboy while the others grow more disheveled and unkempt.

Jack also clashes with Ralph in this chapter, and the tension between their perspectives furthers the novel's concern with the two opposing political ideologies the boys represent, namely, totalitarianism and democracy. Ralph, whose overarching concern is the maintenance of the signal fire, is dedicated to the welfare of the entire group. He uses his power for the good of all. Jack, however, is concerned with becoming a successful hunter, less for the good it will bring to the other boys than for the thrill of the hunt and the increased social status he will have on the island. He seeks power because it will allow him to gratify his impulses and abuse others without punishment. The two boys' treatment of the littluns-Ralph is assuring, while Jack mocks and yells at them-demonstrates their different approaches to power.

The concurrent sighting of the ship and killing of the pig contribute to the disintegration of the relative calm on the island. These two events represent the different strands of human behavior inherent on the island. The ship is a reminder of the civilized society to which the boys belong, renewing the possibility that they may eventually escape the island. The killing of the pig is an example of their descent from civilized behavior into animalistic activity. This makes clear the dichotomy dividing Ralph and Piggy from Jack and the hunters. The former have a greater concern for returning to society while the latter enjoy their freedom from civilization (a group that, again, imposes its own totalitarian order under Jack). This conflict between the two forces at work among the boys on the island will guide much of the following conflict in the novel.

Summary and Analysis of Chapter Five: Beast From Water

Ralph goes to the beach because he needs a place to think and feels overcome with frustration and impotence. He is saddened by his own physical appearance, which has grown shabby with neglect. In particular, his hair has grown uncomfortably long. He understands the weariness of life, where everything requires improvisation. Ralph decides to call a meeting near the bathing pool, realizing that he must think and must make a decision but that he lacks Piggy's natural intellectual ability.

That afternoon, Ralph blows the conch shell and the assembly gathers. He begins the assembly seriously, telling them that they are there not for making jokes or for cleverness. He reminds them that everyone built the first shelter, which is the most sturdy, while the third one, built only by Simon and Ralph, is unstable. He admonishes them for not using the appropriate areas for the lavatory. He also reminds them that the fire is the most important thing on the island, for it is their means of escape. He claims that they ought to die before they let the fire out. He directs this at the hunters in particular. He repeats the rule that the only place where they will have a fire is on the mountain. Addressing the spreading fear among the littluns, Ralph then attempts to demystify the question of the "beastie" or monster. He admits that he is frightened himself, but their fear is unfounded. Ralph again assures the group that there are no monsters on the island.

With his customary abruptness, Jack stands up, takes the conch from Ralph, and begins to yell at the littluns for screaming like babies and not hunting or building or helping. Jack tells them that there is no beast on the island. Piggy does agree with Jack on that point, telling the kids that there are no beasts and there is no real reason for fear-unless it is of other people. A littlun, Phil, tells that he had a nightmare and, when he awoke, saw something big and horrid moving among the trees. Ralph dismisses it as nothing. Simon admits that he was walking in the jungle at night.

Percival speaks next, and as he gives his name he recites his address and telephone number. This reminder of home, however, causes him to break out into tears. All of the littluns join him in crying. Percival claims that the beast comes out of the sea, and he tells them about frightening squids. Simon says that maybe there is a beast, and the boys speak about ghosts. Piggy claims he does not believe in ghosts, but Jack attempts to start a fight again by taunting Piggy and calling him "Fatty." Ralph stops the fight and asks the boys how many of them believe in ghosts. Piggy begins yelling, asking whether the boys are humans, animals, or savages.

Jack threatens Piggy again, and Ralph intercedes once more, complaining that they are breaking the rules. When Jack asks, "who cares?" Ralph says that the rules are the only thing that they have. Jack says that he and his hunters will kill the beast. The assembly breaks up as Jack leads them on a hunt. Only Ralph, Piggy, and Simon remain. Ralph says that if he blows the conch to summon them back and they refuse, then they will become like animals and will never be rescued. He asks Piggy whether there are ghosts or beasts on the island, but Piggy reassures him. Piggy warns Ralph that if he steps down as chief Jack will do nothing but hunt, and they will never be rescued. The three imagine the majesty of adult life. They also hear Percival still sobbing his address.

Analysis

The weight of leadership becomes oppressive for Ralph as the story continues; he is dutiful and dedicated, but his attempts to instill order and calm among the boys are decreasingly successful. Golding develops Ralph's particular concerns and insecurities in this chapter. By showing him brooding over his perceived failures, Golding highlights Ralph's essentially responsible, adult nature. Ralph's concern about his appearance, and particularly his grown-out hair, indicate his natural inclination towards the conventions of civilization. Although Ralph demonstrates a more than sufficient intellect, he also worries that he lacks Piggy's genius. His one consolation is that he realizes that his abilities as a thinker allow him to recognize the same in Piggy, again a rational observation that draws the reader's attention to his potential as a leader. The implication is that deviations from Ralph's plans will be illogical, ill-informed, and dangerous.

Ralph still has a strong sense of self-doubt. He is not immune to fear, which he admits to the boys, and he even feels it necessary to ask Piggy whether there might actually be a ghost on the island. Thus, Golding presents Ralph as a reluctant leader. His elected position of chief has been thrust upon him, and he assumes it only because he is the most natural and qualified leader. He has no real ambition or drive, such as the rapacious energy that motivates Jack, but he knows that the boys will be best provided for under his care. It is Ralph who is most concerned with the rules of order on the island. He accurately tells the boys that without the rules, the boys have nothing. Ralph's rules keep the boys tethered to some semblance of society, but without these rules there will be disastrous consequences.

Piggy remains the only fully rational character during the assembly and afterward. Piggy is the only boy who categorically dismisses the idea of a beast on the island, and he even reassures the generally unwavering Ralph on this point. It is Piggy who realizes that the boys' fear is the only danger that they truly face so long as they have enough food to survive, and even this fear proves no actual threat to them. Still, the outcast Piggy once again is ignored in favor of lurid tales of beasts and ghosts; although he is consistently correct in his judgments, Piggy is continually ignored. He raises the important question of whether the boys wish to act like humans, savages, or animals. Once again, Ralph and Piggy exemplify civilized human order, while Jack represents a brutal anarchy that may devolve into animal behavior.

The conflict between Jack and Ralph, with Piggy as his ally, reaches a breaking point in this chapter. Although Jack initially dismisses the idea of a beast on the island, he comes to accept the idea when they conceive of the beast as an enemy that his hunters may kill. Jack continues to be an aggressive and destructive force. He again physically threatens Piggy, foreshadowing the eventual violent conflict between the two boys, and he even manipulates the young boys' fear of monsters and ghosts. During the assembly Jack fully abandons the rules and codes of society. He promotes anarchy among the boys, leading them on a disorganized hunt for an imaginary beast. While Ralph is appointed leader for his calm demeanor and rationality, Jack gains his authority from irrationality and instinctual fear, manipulating the boys into thinking that there may be a dangerous creature that they should hunt. This behavior is dangerous; Ralph concludes that a focus on hunting will prevent them from ever leaving the island and seal their fate as no more than animals.

The assembly highlights how fear ferments and spreads in a group. The littluns begin with a concrete example of a frightening incident that is easily explained and is understandable, but the idea of something more sinister on the island provokes mass hysteria. The terrors that the boys imagine become progressively more abstract and threatening. Percival uses concrete facts about squids to arrive at an illogical conclusion that a squid may emerge from the sea to harm them. This then provokes the unfounded rumors that there may be supernatural beings, ghosts, on the island.

Monsters, violent squid, and ghosts: all three creatures represent different instantiations of the "beast" or "beastie" that has been the subject of the boys' mounting fear. As the title suggests, the beast is of crucial importance to this chapter and will figure largely in the tragic events to come. On a symbolic level, the beast has several meanings. First, it invokes the devil, the Satan of Judeo-Christian mythology, which foreshadows the "lord of the flies" object that will become the mascot of Jack's tribe later. The fear of the beast among the boys may symbolize their fear of evil from an external, supernatural source. Second, it symbolizes the unknown, amoral, dark forces of nature, which remain beyond the boys' control. Finally, the beast may allude to the Freudian concept of the Id, the instinctual, primordial drive that is present in the human psyche and which, unfettered by social mores, tends towards savagery and destruction. In this framework, the boys' fear of the beast is a displacement of a fear of themselves, of their capacity for violence and evil which is unleashed in the absence of adult authority and ordered social life.

With the anarchy incited by Jack and the panic among the littluns, only the illusion of civilization is left on the island. Percival's tearful repetition of his home address is a stark reminder that the boys no longer reside in civilized culture and that the Home Counties remain little more than a pleasant memory. As Ralph, Piggy, and Simon muse on adulthood, we recall that adult society should be sufficiently rational and organized to solve the problems that the children face on the island, though we wonder how well a similar group of adults would do.

Summary and Analysis of Chapter Six: Beast from Air

Later that night, Ralph and Simon pick up Percival and carry him into a shelter. Overhead, beyond the horizon, there is an aerial battle while the boys sleep. They do not hear the explosions in the sky, nor do they see a pilot drop from a parachute, sweeping across the reef toward the mountain. Unbeknownst to the boys, the dead pilot lands on the mountaintop, his flapping chute throwing strange shadows across the ground, with his head appearing to float in the wind.

Early the next morning, there are noises from a rock falling down the side of the mountain. The twins Samneric, the two boys on duty at the fire, awake and add kindling to the fire. Just then they spot the dead pilot at the top of the mountain and are immobilized by fear. Eventually, they scramble down the mountain to wake Ralph. Samneric claim that they saw the beast. Ralph calls a meeting, and the group assembles again at the beach. Eric announces to the other boys that he and Sam saw the beast. He describes it as having teeth and claws and states that it followed them as they ran away.

Jack calls for a hunt, but Piggy says that they should stay there, for the beast may not want to approach them on the beach. In response to Jack's belligerence, Piggy points out that only he has the right to speak because he is holding the conch. Jack responds that they no longer need the conch. Ralph becomes exasperated at Jack, accusing him of not wanting to be rescued, and Jack takes a swing at him. Despite Jack's hostility towards Ralph and the rules of the island, Ralph not only allows Jack to lead the hunt but also decides that he will accompany the hunters to search for the beast.

Simon, wanting to prove that he is accepted, travels with Ralph, who wishes only for solitude. Soon, they reach a part of the island that they had not yet discovered. It is a thin path that leads to a series of caves inside a mountain face. While the other boys are afraid to traverse the walkway and explore the caves, Ralph accomplishes the feat and is encouraged by his own bravery. He enters one of the caves and is soon joined by Jack. The two experience a brief reconciliation as they have fun together exploring the new mountain territory.

They continue along a narrow wall of rocks that forms a bridge between parts of the island, reaching the open sea. At this point, however, some of the boys get distracted and spend time rolling rocks around the bridge. Ralph again gets frustrated and then asserts that it would be better to climb the mountain and rekindle the fire. He accuses the boys of losing sight of their original goal, finding and killing the beast. Contradicting Ralph, Jack states that he wishes to stay where they are because they can build a fort.

Analysis

The landing of the dead pilot on the mountain is a pivotal event in Lord of the Flies. The pilot represents an actual manifestation of the beast whose existence the boys had feared but never confirmed. None of the boys is immune to the implications of the dead pilot's presence on the island. Even Piggy, faced with some evidence that a beast actually exists, begins considering measures the boys should take to protect themselves. In contrast to the "beast from water" of the previous chapter (alternately figured as a monster, squid, and ghost), the beast from air is a concrete object toward which the boys can direct their fear. Significantly, however, the beast from air proves no threat to the boys. The dead body is nothing more than a harmless object left to be interpreted in vastly different ways by the various boys.

Given his increasingly violent behavior, intensified further by his successful slaughter of a forest pig, Jack unsurprisingly interprets the appearance of the beast from air as a cause for war. The possibility of a dangerous presence on the island is key to Jack's gaining authority over the other boys, for he affirms their fear and gives them a focus for their violence and anger. Jack thus continues his authoritarian behavior with a strong emphasis on demagoguery. Jack requires a concrete enemy in order to assume dictatorial authority, and he finds one in the dead pilot despite its obvious inability to harm them. This foreshadows later developments in which Jack will focus his vitriol against other possible enemies. Like many tyrants, Jack assumes power by directing public fear towards scapegoats, in this case, the body of the dead pilot.

Chapter Six also confirms the increasing tension between Jack and Ralph, whose opposing ideas of social organization resurface. While he despises Piggy, Jack's most threatening enemy is Ralph, who insists on rules and self-discipline over wild adventures and hunting. Ralph remains focused on the clear objective of keeping the fire burning to alert possible passing ships, while Jack is committed to only those pursuits that allow him to behave in a destructive manner. Previously, Jack was committed to the rules of order that would allow him to punish others; in this chapter, however, Golding presents Jack as accepting anarchy when it serves his purposes. His assertion that the boys no longer need the conch shell in meetings signifies Jack's explicit rejection of the democratic rules established in the boys' first meeting. Jack emerges in Chapter Six as driven less by totalitarian or anarchist ideology than by self-interest, although the anarchy makes room for a new order led totally by Jack.

Jack's increasing credibility among the group isolates Ralph from the other boys, who find Jack's focus on the games of hunting and building forts more appealing than Ralph's commitment to keeping the fire burning and remaining safe. After all, what is so bad about a life on the beach with plenty of fruit and fun? Throughout the chapter, Golding develops this rift between the more mature Ralph and the other boys. Ralph finds he must ally himself with the intellectual Piggy and the introspective Simon. As the other boys narrow their focus to pure self-interest, with a limited focus on survival (killing the beast) and a greater goal of satisfying their boyish desires (playing as hunters), the three boys represent three facets of distinctly human thought. Ralph, who strives to balance priorities successfully, represents practical reason and democratic ethics. Piggy the problem-solver represents pure intellect. Simon, in contrast, is a spiritual thinker who demonstrates the ability to transcend individual interests in order to achieve not just peace but harmony with others and with the natural environment.

Significantly, Golding begins Chapter Six with a description of an aerial battle that, unlike most of the narrative, is not filtered through one of the boys' perspectives. The reader learns of the events of the battle while the boys remain sleeping and unaware. This special knowledge calls our attention to the dramatic irony here, the gap between reality and the boys' interpretation of that reality. The group's hysterical reaction to the "beast from air," which the reader knows is a dead parachutist, underscores how distorted, irrational, and fear-driven the boys' reasoning is. Rather than leaving readers with the boys' perspective, which would require readers to figure out the reality of the situation on their own, Golding briefly gives the reader an objective viewpoint in order to help readers perceive the danger of the children's mounting irrationality.

Moreover, the chapter's opening description of the aerial battle highlights one of the novel's missions, that is, as a political allegory rooted in the Cold War. The war described here is fictional and accords with no real historical events; nevertheless, the rhetoric Golding uses in this section evokes the conflict of the Cold War. The battle is between England and "the Reds," and an atom bomb-the main weapon at issue in the arms race-is responsible for evacuating the children from the Home Counties. Golding plays on the fears of Cold War America and Great Britain to reinforce his cautionary tale about the superiority of democracy. That the war again threatens the boys, through the misinterpreted figure of the dead parachutist, also draws the reader's attention to the fact that the children are primarily victims of war. From this perspective, the tragic events to follow are consequences of a global crisis rooted as much in war as in human nature.

Again in Chapter Six, Golding uses religious symbolism to express the underlying themes of the novel. The dead parachutist appears to the boys as a supernatural creature; Golding enforces the twins' interpretation by describing the dead body with mystical imagery and language. The body appears to lift and drop its own head, and the flapping parachute opens and closes in the wind. Samneric describe it as a "beast," but Golding's opening description, which follows the parachutist as he drifts across the island-as well as the wing-like quality of his torn parachute-implies that he is more akin to a fallen angel. In Judeo-Christian mythology the first fallen angel was Lucifer, who later became Satan, the incarnation of evil. The parachutist thus serves as a symbol of, and motivation for, the evil that is now manifesting on the island. The Satanic function of the dead body is compounded by the violent, tragic action that results from the confusion surrounding its identity.

Summary and Analysis of Chapter Seven: Shadows and Tall Trees

The boys continue to travel across the island to the mountain, and they stop to eat. Ralph notices how long his hair is and how dirty and unclean he has become. He has been following the hunters, and he observes that on this side of the island, which is opposite to the one on which the boys have settled, the view is utterly different. The horizon is a hard, clipped blue, and the ocean crashes against the rocks. He compares the ocean to a thick wall, an impermeable barrier preventing the boys' escape. As Ralph appears to lose hope, Simon reassures him that they will leave the island eventually. Ralph is somewhat doubtful, but Simon replies that his thoughts are simply opinions. Roger calls for Ralph, telling him that they need to continue hunting.

That afternoon, the boys discover pig droppings. Jack suggests that they hunt the pig in addition to continuing their search for the beast. A boar appears, and the boys set out in pursuit of it. Ralph, who has never hunted before, is excited by the chase and quickly gets caught up in the adventure. He throws his spear at a boar. While it only nicks his snout, Ralph is encouraged by what he considers his good marksmanship.

Jack is wounded on his left forearm, apparently by the boar's tusks. He proudly presents his wound to the crowd, and Simon tells him he should suck the wound to prevent infection. The hunters go into a frenzy once more, repeatedly chanting "kill the pig." Caught up in the momentum of their chanting and dancing, they jab at Robert with their spears, at first in jest, and then with more dangerous intent. Frightened and hurt, Robert drags himself away from the crowd, now aware that they are carried away with their game. Roger and Jack talk about the chanting, and Jack says that someone should dress up as a pig and pretend to knock him over. When Robert says that Jack should get a real pig that he can actually kill, Jack replies that they could just use a littlun. The boys, enamored by Jack's bold statement, laugh and cheer him on. Ralph tries to remind the boys that they were only playing a game. He is concerned about the increasingly violent, impulsive behavior of the hunters.

As evening falls, the boys start climbing up the mountain once more, and Ralph realizes that they won't be able to return to the beach until morning. He does not want to leave the littluns alone with Piggy all night. Jack mocks Ralph for his concern for Piggy. Simon says that he can go back to the beach and inform the group of the hunters' whereabouts. Ralph tells Jack that there is not enough light to go hunting for pigs, so they should wait until morning. Sensing hostility from Jack, Ralph asks him why he hates him. Jack has no answer.

Though the hunters are tired and afraid, Jack vows that he will go up the mountain to look for the beast. Jack mocks Ralph for not wanting to go up the mountain, accusing him of being afraid. Jack claims he saw something bulge on the mountain. Since Jack seems for the first time somewhat afraid, Ralph agrees that they will look for it immediately. The boys see a rock-like hump and something like a great ape sitting asleep with its head between its knees. As soon as they see it, the boys run off, terrified.

Analysis

In this chapter, Golding further develops the themes he introduced in "Beast From Air." The rift between Jack and Ralph becomes more intense as Ralph continues to remind Jack of his misguided priorities. The struggle in this chapter between the two characters again assumes political overtones, as the two engage in a power struggle for authority over the other boys. The concerns of Ralph and Jack were established in previous chapters: the former focuses on survival and escape while the latter focuses on hunting and self-gratification. In this chapter Golding examines the tactics that each uses to assert his authority. Jack uses his bravado to signify his strength and dominance, and he attempts to diminish Ralph in the eyes of the other boys by ridiculing him for his supposed cowardice. Ralph, on the other hand, is straightforward and direct. He challenges Jack's overblown self-confidence by honestly noting that Jack is wrongly motivated by hatred.

Golding continues to use imagery and symbolism to trace the boys' descent into disorder, violence, and amorality. In particular, Golding suggests in this chapter that the line between the boys and animals is becoming increasingly blurred. The hunters chant and dance, and one of the boys again pretends to be a pig while the other boys pretend to kill him. The parallel between boy and pig in the ritual is a powerful dramatization of the implications of the boys' giving in to their violent impulses, indicating that the children are no better than animals and that, like the pig, they too will be sacrificed to fulfill the brutal desires of Jack and his hunters.

Characterization in Chapter Seven also foreshadows the tragic events to come. In particular, Jack, who is increasingly confident as a hunter and leader, suggests that his violent impulses are now directed at the other children as well as at the pigs on the island. Jack's joke that the group should kill a littlun in place of a pig demonstrates a blatant disregard for human life and explicitly acknowledges that he appreciates violence for its own sake. His joke also signals the waning of his conscience as the boys continue to exist in the absence of adult society and its rules. Jack, who previously needed to prepare himself to kill a pig, indicates that he is now probably capable of killing people without remorse.

As Ralph faces the challenge of tracking and hunting the beast, physical tasks that are unfamiliar to him as the political leader of the boys, he demonstrates the dangerous appeal of aggressive and impulsive behavior such as Jack's. Golding tracks Ralph's brief sympathy with Jack's mindset to suggest that even the most civilized humans are susceptible to groupthink and the pressures of the Id, which is inclined towards destruction and self-gratification. The chapter begins with Ralph expressing disgust over his appearance, which again indicates his natural disinclination towards savagery. Yet, like Jack, Ralph feels exhilarated during the hunt and begins to understand the primal appeal of killing pigs. It is Jack's decision to continue the hunt in darkness, which Ralph rightly recognizes as ill-informed, that finally reminds Ralph of the essential foolishness of Jack's mindset. By showing Ralph's character as threatened but not subsumed by Jack's will, Golding suggests that the human impulse towards savagery, which is both strong and natural, can nevertheless be overcome by reason and intelligence.

While Golding's characterization of Jack and his hunters intends to caution the reader about the destructive impulses that reside inside all humans, it is important to note the historical biases at work in this depiction of the boys' hunting rituals. The boys chant and dance around in circles, whipping themselves up into a "frenzy" that pushes them to the brink of actual murder. They represent or are becoming "savages," which in Golding's time reminded readers of the native peoples of the Americas and Africa. This stereotype tended to associate these peoples with a very limited and barbaric culture, failing to appreciate the complex culture that events such as ritual dances expressed. A more charitable view of Jack's new warrior culture, say from an anthropologist's perspective, would not stress the dehumanization of the war-dance so much as their natural human reaction to the difficult conditions on the island, a reaction that after all can produce the meat that the children need.

Nature is also of crucial significance in this chapter. As the boys move farther from the camp into the unexplored recesses of the forest and mountain areas, they contend with the powerful forces of the natural world, which is untamed and indifferent to the boys' concerns. The emphasis on the indifference of nature in this chapter is significant in several ways. First, it suggests the continuing dehumanization of the boys as they remain cut off from the larger world and without successful social organization. Their progress from the semi-humanized beach, with its shelters and sandcastles, to the wild forest and mountain areas, mirrors their descent into complete savagery. The chapter's beginning, in which Ralph compares the ocean to an impenetrable wall, also suggests the extent to which nature remains the boys' most powerful antagonist. Ralph's pessimistic observations foreshadow the following chapters, in which Simon discovers that the "beast" is actually a dead body, whose presence on the island can be explained rationally. It was the darkness of the night that prevented the boys from recognizing the true nature of the creature of the mountaintop. Throughout the novel, the natural world frustrates and threatens the boys' understanding of their situation and their relationships with one another. Ralph's sense of defeat in the face of the ocean in this chapter thus indicates that he is beginning to register the power of nature and the part it plays in their struggle for rescue and self-government.

The conclusion of the chapter, with the boys' collective misrecognition of the dead parachutist as a malevolent beast, highlights the power of human nature to fear the unknown and magnify its importance. The boys compare the figure on the mountaintop to a great ape. The primate is a common symbol for early man and man's origins as an animal species. The boys recognize the ape-like creature as a monster, a moment that underscores the monstrous potential of humanity at its most primitive and base. The parachutist, whose arrival on the island inaugurates a series of events that lead to complete anarchy and bloodshed, thus links together evil, nature, and humanity in a single symbol. The haste with which the boys decide the dead body is a "monster" indicates not only the infectiousness of hysterical thinking among the boys, but also the extent to which the beast is a projection of their fear of their own savagery and violence.

Summary and Analysis of Chapter Eight: Gift for the Darkness

The next morning, the boys gather on the beach to discuss what the hunters saw. Ralph tells Piggy about the creature on the mountain, which he describes as a beast with teeth and big black eyes. Piggy is skeptical. Jack assures the group that his hunters can defeat the beast, but Ralph dismisses Jack's group as no more than boys with sticks. Jack tells the other boys that the beast is a hunter, and he informs them that Ralph thinks that the boys are cowards. He continues his attack on Ralph, claiming that Ralph is no proper chief, for he is a coward himself. Jack asks the boys if they want Ralph to be fired as chief. When nobody agrees with him, Jack runs off in tears. He asserts that he is no longer going to be part of Ralph's lot. Jack leaves the group on the beach.

After Jack runs off, Piggy tells the group they can do without him, but they should stay close to the platform. Simon suggests that they climb the mountain. Piggy says that if they climb the mountain they can start the fire again, but he then suggests that they start a fire down by the beach. Piggy organizes the new fire area by the beach. Ralph notices that several of the boys are missing. Piggy is confident that they all will do well enough if they behave with common sense, and he proposes a feast. They wonder where Simon has gone and surmise that he might be climbing the mountain. In fact, Simon left to sit in the open space he had found earlier.

Far off along the beach, Jack proclaims that he will be chief of the hunters and that they must forget about the beast. He says that they might go later to the castle rock, but now they will kill a pig and have a feast to celebrate their independence. They find a group of pigs, and Jack kills a large sow by forcing his spear up her anus. Jack rubs the blood over Maurice's cheeks while Roger laughs about how the fatal blow against the sow was delivered up her ass. They cut off the pig's head and leave it on a stick as a gift for the beast at the mountaintop. When they place the offering upright, blood drips down the sow's teeth, and they run away. Simon, from his private space, sees the head, which has flies buzzing around it.

Back on the beach, Ralph worries that the boys will die if they are not rescued soon. Ralph and Piggy realize that it is Jack who makes everything break apart.

Ralph's group is startled as the forest suddenly bursts into uproar. The littluns run off while Jack approaches, naked except for paint and a belt, his hunters taking burning branches from the fire. Jack tells Ralph and his group that he and his hunters are living along the beach by a flat rock, where they hunt and feast and have fun. He invites the boys to join his tribe. When Jack leaves, Ralph says that he thought Jack was going to take the conch, which Ralph still considers a symbol of ritual and order. They reassure each other again that the fire is the most important task at hand. But a boy among them named Bill appears skeptical. He suggests that they go to the hunters' feast and tell them that the fire is hard on them. At the top of the mountain remains the pig's head, which Simon has dubbed the Lord of the Flies.

Simon believes that the pig's head speaks to him. He thinks that it is calling him a silly little boy. The Lord of the Flies tells Simon to run off and play with the others, who think that he is crazy. The Lord of the Flies claims that he is the Beast, and the Beast laughs at the idea that the Beast is something that could be hunted and killed, for he is within every human being and thus can never be defeated or escaped from. Terrified and disoriented by this disturbing vision, Simon falls down and loses consciousness.

Analysis

In this chapter, Golding continues to use his main characters as personifications of various facets of the human spirit. Piggy remains the lone skeptic among the boys and still unsure of the presence of the beast, which continues to be the focus of island life for Jack and his hunters. Even Ralph, succumbing to fear and suspicion, now believes that there is a beast on the island. Although Ralph is the clear protagonist of the story and the character to whom Golding affixes the reader's perspective, he is still susceptible to the childish passions and irrationality that are, to varying extents, present in the other children. Ralph's weakness is not insignificant. While Ralph may be more mature and rational than Jack and his hunters, given the right circumstances he can submit to the same passions as the other boys, a tendency that foreshadows the tragic events that unfold in subsequent chapters.

The political subtext of previous chapters becomes more overt in this chapter as Jack explicitly attempts to overthrow Ralph as chief. Although Ralph successfully defends himself against Jack's attack by calling the other boys' attention to Jack's shortsightedness and cowardice, Jack is resolved that he will take control. Jack's refusal to accept the other boys' decision serves as a reminder that Jack is still a child who considers life on the island as a game; he assumes the position that, if he cannot set the rules of the game, he refuses to play at all. This decision provokes the subsequent events of the chapter, which focus on Jack's rejection not only of Ralph's authority but of the entire pseudo-democracy on the island that had conferred authority on Ralph. Jack, realizing that he cannot take authority directly away from Ralph, appoints himself as the authority and begins his own "tribe." Two "governments" thus exist on the island in this chapter. Ralph presides over what resembles a liberal democracy, while Jack forms a type of military dictatorship. The two systems remain ideologically opposed, an opposition that Golding highlights by placing the camps on different sides of the island. The structure of the chapter also evokes the creation of two different governments on the island and foreshadows the dominance of Jack's system over Ralph's. If there is a belligerent culture nearby, a peaceful culture must militarize in order to survive. The chapter begins with Jack rejecting Ralph's conch shell as a symbol of authority conferred by democratic consensus, and it ends with the creation of the Lord of the Flies, a symbol of the lawlessness and violence that motivates Jack's desire for power.

Golding also continues to represent Piggy as the sensible and in some respects the most essential character for the boys' survival. The abrasive edge that Piggy demonstrated upon their arrival now becomes secondary to his practical wisdom, his ability to quickly understand and adapt to new situations. Among the major characters, Piggy is the only one who does not have predictable emotions. While Jack and Simon descend into their respective forms of madness and Ralph remains sensible but increasingly cynical and vulnerable, Piggy confounds the reader's expectations by assuming authority over the boys despite his sickly appearance and aversion to physical labor. In this chapter, even Ralph defers to Piggy's sound judgment and resolve. But any hints of Piggy's heroism in this chapter are undermined by the increasing subjugation of the island's pigs to Jack and his hunters. Piggy is linked to the pigs by his name; as Jack's group become more focused on and adept at hunting them, Piggy's own victimization by the group becomes more likely. In part, the killing of the sow foreshadows Piggy's tragic fate.

As was foreshadowed in the previous chapter, Jack and his hunters continue to devolve into savagery in Chapter Eight. They indulge more and more in stereotypical "native" behavior that emphasizes the use of violence and rituals of song and dance. For these boys the actions are initially little more than a game; when Jack invites the other boys to join his tribe, he explains that the point of this new tribe is solely to have fun. The boys continue to see their behavior as savages as part of an elaborate game, even as the "game" takes on increasingly dangerous and violent undertones. The mounting brutality and impulsiveness of Jack's group in this chapter foreshadows the events of Chapter Nine, in which the boys' behavior moves from mere pretending at violence to actual murder.

The scene where Simon confronts the pig's head, which he calls the Lord of the Flies, remains the most debated episode among critics of the novel. Many critics have noted that the scene resembles the New Testament's telling of Jesus' confrontation with Satan during his forty days in the wilderness. Simon, a naturally moral, selfless character, does seem to be a Christ-figure who, in his knowledge of the true nature of the beast, is the sole bearer of truth at this point in the novel. In this scene with the pig's head, represented as evil, he meets and struggles against his antithesis. His eventual sacrifice, again an allusion to the crucifixion of Jesus, will mark the triumph of evil over good on the island.

A close reading of Simon's interaction with the pig's head can yield additional interpretations. In ways that complicate the biblical allegory in this scene, Golding also represents the Lord of the Flies in this chapter as the symbol of the boys' descent from civilized behavior to inhuman savagery. In this framework, the pig's head serves as a corrective for Simon's naive view of nature as a peaceful force. For Simon, the pig's head is a revelation (his final one) that alerts him to the fact that while nature is beautiful and fascinating, it is also brutal and indifferent. In previous chapters, Golding linked Simon to a vision of nature that was abundant, beautiful, and Edenic. The Lord of the Flies represents a different kind of nature, a hellish one, not one of paradise. Seen through Simon's perspective, the Lord of the Flies is a

Hobbesian reminder that human life in the most basic state of nature is in fact nasty, brutish, short, and worse. In keeping with Golding's characterization of Simon as spiritual, the pig's head has deep religious connotations: the phrase "lord of the flies" is a translation of the Hebrew word Ba'alzevuv, or its Greek equivalent Beelzebub. The pig's head is thus a symbol of Satan, but, as it reminds Simon, this devil is not an external force. Rather, it is a more nefarious evil, one created by, and remaining within, the boys themselves.

Another interesting facet of Golding's representation of nature in this chapter is evident in the pig hunt. Historically, artists and novelists have associated the natural world with women, in contrast to the civilized world, which they linked to men. Nature is often gendered in literature as female and in this sense a threat to the civilized forces of masculinity. Accordingly, Golding represents this pig hunt in gendered terms and with violent sexual imagery in that the boys kill a female pig with a spear thrust into her anus, which evokes rape. In a novel that has no female human characters appearing in any scene, and in which women are barely even mentioned, this sow and what happens to her carries additional weight. The brutal murder of the sow represents the boys' attempts to subjugate and impose their will on the natural world, coded here as feminine. We may again note the metaphoric link between Piggy and the sow, which calls attention to the ways in which Piggy is himself coded as "feminine": hairless, softly rounded, and with several stereotypically girlish qualities, such as disliking physical labor. In this way, too, the sow's subjugation anticipates his own.

Summary and Analysis of Chapter Nine: A View to a Death

On the humid, dark mountaintop, Simon's fit passes into the weariness of sleep. Waking up, Simon speaks aloud to himself, questioning what he will do next. His nose bleeding, he climbs farther up the mountain, and in the dim light, catches sight of the Beast. This time, however, he recognizes it as the body of the man who parachuted onto the island. Overwhelmed with disgust and dread, Simon vomits. He realizes that he must inform the other boys of their mistake, and he staggers down the mountain toward Jack's camp to tell them what he has found.

Ralph notices the clouds overhead and estimates that it will rain again. Ralph and Piggy play in the lagoon, and Piggy gets mad when Ralph squirts water on him, getting his glasses wet. They wonder where most of the other boys have gone, and they realize that they must have gone to Jack's feast for the childish fun of pretending to be a tribe and putting on war paint. They decide to find them to ensure that the events do not spiral out of control.

When Ralph and Piggy arrive at Jack's camp, they find the other boys sitting in a group together, laughing and eating the roasted sow. Jack, now a leader, sits on a great log, painted and garlanded as an idol. When he sees Ralph and Piggy, he orders the other boys to give them something to eat, then orders another boy to bring him a drink. Jack asks all of the boys who among them will join his tribe, for he gave them food and demonstrated that his hunters will protect them. Ralph is distressed to see most of them agree to join Jack's tribe. Attempting to convince his boys otherwise, Ralph provokes yet another argument with Jack, and the two yell at each other about who deserves to be chief. Feeling that he is losing ground, Ralph appeals to his symbol of authority, the conch shell. Jack, however, does not acknowledge the conch's significance and tells Ralph that it does not count on his side of the island.

Disturbed by the hostile turn of events, Piggy urges Ralph to leave Jack's camp before there is serious trouble. It starts to rain. Ralph warns the group that a storm is coming and points out that Jack's tribe is unprepared for such disasters, since they do not even have any shelters. The littluns become frightened, and Jack tries to reassure them by ordering his group to perform its ritual pig hunting dance. The boys begin dancing and chanting wildly, and they are soon consumed by frenzy. The storm begins, and a figure emerges suddenly from the forest. It is Simon, running to tell the others about the dead parachutist. Caught up in the madness of the dance, however, they do not recognize him. As Simon cries out about the dead body on the mountain, the boys rush after him with violent malice. They fall on Simon, striking him repeatedly until he is dead.

Meanwhile, on the mountain, the storm intensifies and spreads across the island. The boys run to the shelters, seeking safety from the increasingly violent wind and rain. The strong winds lift the parachute and the body attached to it and blow it across the island and into the sea, a sight which again terrifies the boys, who still mistake the body for a beast. At the same time, the strong tide, propelled by wind, washes over Simon's body and carries it out to sea, where a school of glowing fish surrounds it.

Analysis

In this particularly significant chapter, Ralph finally loses his leadership over the other boys, who succumb to Jack's increasing charisma and the opportunity he gives them to indulge their violent and childish interests. Golding underscores the tragedy of this shift in power with the violent storm that ravages the island, a storm for which the shortsighted Jack was not prepared. Just when Ralph's calm judgment and practicality is most needed, he lacks the authority to bring the boys to safety. The storm on the island serves as a reminder of the perils they face; while Ralph has built shelters for the boys and is prepared for this situation, Jack has focused simply on hunting and entertaining the boys, to their detriment. Golding again directs the reader's sympathy towards Ralph, whose concern remains for the good of the group.

Jack's authority over the other boys becomes increasingly disturbing and dangerous in this chapter. When Ralph finds Jack, he is painted and garlanded, sitting on a log like an idol. This distinctly pagan image is at odds with the ordered society from which Jack came and is the final manifestation of his rejection of civilization. We may note again the presence of chanting and dancing among the boys in his group and recall that, prior to their arrival on the island, Jack and his boys were members of a choir. Traditionally, boys' choirs sang Christian religious songs and hymns. Jack and his tribesmen still sing, but they sing chants that strongly evoke the animistic religious traditions of native cultures. Their choice of ritual and song, coupled with Jack's appearance as an "idol," indicates the boys' complete and final rejection of the civilization of the Home Counties.

In this chapter, Golding also emphasizes Jack's rise to power and foreshadows the brutal consequences of his authority. Again, Jack rejects the rules established for the island, telling Ralph that the conch yields no authority when Ralph attempts to cite precedent. He signifies his power over his tribe with his painted body and garlands, an image that alludes to Joseph Conrad's 1902 novella, Heart of Darkness, in which a boat captain, Marlow, accepts an assignment to find a defecting government agent, Kurtz, in Africa. In Conrad's story, Marlow discovers Kurtz in a remote area of the continent, living with a group of natives who worship him as their leader and god. In this chapter of Lord of the Flies, Golding draws a deliberate parallel between Jack and Kurtz in order to emphasize the extent of Jack's power over the other boys and to call the reader's attention to the severity of the tension between Ralph and Jack which, like the tension between Marlow and Kurtz, is strongly ideological (Marlow and Ralph representing civilization, and Jack and Kurtz representing savagery). This tension eventually leads to violent conflict.

Note the increasing importance of the beast to the boys in this chapter, and its centrality to Jack's usurping of leadership from Ralph. As Ralph and Piggy discover,

Jack and his tribe have constructed an elaborate mythology around the beast, to whom they now attribute many qualities that were not present in earlier descriptions. They believe that the beast is immortal and can change shape as it wishes, and they claim that it must be both worshiped and feared. Around this mythology Jack has established the rules of his society. His boys are united by their belief in the beast and, above this, their belief in Jack as the one person who can protect them from the beast. Their ritual dances and chants, as well as Jack's makeup and adornments, express their commitment to this mythology, within which the Lord of the Flies functions totemically.

The Lord of the Flies embodies and expresses the mythology of the beast that unites Jack's tribe and is significant in many ways. As an offering to the body of the parachutist on the mountain, which the boys (excluding Piggy) regard as the beast, it symbolizes Jack's acknowledgment of, and deferral to, the evil impulses that reside inside the individual psyche. In previous chapters, he had vowed to kill the beast; here, Jack attempts to appease it, to gain its favor. As a totem, an artifact that unites Jack's tribe (much like the conch served as a totem for Ralph's group), the Lord of the Flies symbolizes the solidification of Jack's group around a shared set of values and interests which, as we have noted, are self-interested and indulgent. Finally, as a memento of the hunting of the sow, the Lord of the Flies represents the imposition of human will over nature, another of Jack's goals for island life. The pig's head reminds the boys of the essential opposition between man and nature, an opposition Jack views as essentially hostile and one that the boys can win.

The most important event of the chapter, however, is the murder of Simon by Jack's tribe. They are in a trance-like state from their ritual dancing, although this does not excuse them. The murder continues the parallel between Simon and Jesus established in the previous chapter by depicting the murder as a sacrifice, akin to Christ's murder on the cross. Like Jesus, who was the sole bearer of knowledge of God's will, it is Simon who alone possesses the truth about the beast. Also like Christ's, Simon's tragedy is governed by the fact that he is misunderstood or disbelieved by those around him. For example, the other boys believe Simon is crazy, yet he is the only boy to discover the truth about the supposed beast. This irony is compounded when Jack's hunters mistake Simon for the beast himself. His murder represents the culmination of the violent tendencies prevalent among Jack's band of hunters, who finally move from brutality against animals to brutality against each other. The change is subtle: they murder Simon out of instinct, descending on him before they realize that he proves no danger to them. Nevertheless, this is yet another line that the boys cross on their devolution into inhuman savagery and another step toward engaging in complete and premeditated violence against one another. Simon's murder reveals the essential brutality of the human spirit. On both metaphoric and structural levels, Golding casts Simon as a martyr, a figure whose death is instructive at least to the reader.

The parallels between Simon and Christ continue even after Simon is dead. We may note not only the religious subtext of the chapter's final image, but the distinctly pessimistic tone of this subtext. The storm simultaneously removes the parachutist's and Simon's bodies from the island. Yet, while the parachutist appears to ascend on the winds, Simon is dragged under the tide. The parachutist, who represents both the war that caused the events that brought the children to the island (he is a soldier) and, in a more general sense, the evil that is present in the human psyche (he resembles a fallen angel, a common figure for Satan), is lifted into the sky, while Simon, a Christ-like figure, appears to descend beneath the surface of the earth. The image, therefore, reverses the traditional story, with Satan rising to the heavens and Christ descending to the underworld. The implication is that the ideal order of good and evil has been reversed on the island. Evil has triumphed, a suggestion that mirrors Jack's rise to power and foreshadows the even more tragic events to come. Still, a vestige of optimism remains: Simon's body, as it is carried out to sea, is surrounded by some small glowing fish, who function as a kind of living halo. They do not necessarily want to eat the body; perhaps they are figuratively honoring it. The implication is that the truth of Simon's message, and the injustice of his death, will be recognized in time, as is the case with martyred prophets and saints.

Summary and Analysis of Chapter Ten: The Shell and the Glasses

Back on the other side of the island, Ralph and Piggy meet on the beach. Tired, injured, and disturbed by the previous night's action, they discuss Simon. Piggy reminds Ralph that he is still chief, or at least chief over those who are still with them. Piggy tries to stop Ralph from dwelling on Simon's murder by appealing to Ralph's reason. Piggy says that he participated in the murder because he was scared, to which Ralph replies that he was not scared. He does not know what came over him. Piggy tries to justify the death as an accident provoked by Simon's "crazy" behavior, but Ralph, clutching the conch defensively, is consumed with guilt and regret and insists that they took part in a murder.

Piggy asks Ralph not to reveal to Samneric that they were involved in Simon's death. Ralph and Piggy reveal that almost all the other boys have abandoned them for Jack's tribe save Samneric and some other littluns. Samneric return to the beach, where they present Ralph and Piggy with a log they have dragged out of the forest. They immediately take off to go swimming. Ralph stops the twins with the intention of informing them that he and Piggy did not participate in Simon's murder. All four appear nervous as they discuss where they were the previous night, trying to avoid the subject of Simon's murder. All insist that they left early, right after the feast.

At Castle Rock, Roger is attempting to gain entry to Jack's camp. Robert, already inside, makes Roger announce himself before he can enter-one of Jack's new rules. When Roger enters, Robert shows him a new feature of Jack's camp: the boys have rigged a log so that they can easily trigger a rock to tumble down and crush whatever is below it. Roger appears disturbed by this, and Robert changes the subject, telling him that Jack had a boy named Wilfred tied up for no apparent reason. Roger considers the implications of Jack's "irresponsible authority" and makes his way back down to the caves and the other boys in Jack's tribe. He finds Jack sitting on a log, nearly naked with a painted face. Jack declares to the group that tomorrow they will hunt again. He warns them about the beast and about intruders. He promises them another feast. Reluctantly, Bill asks Jack what they will use to light the fire. Jack blushes. He finally answers that they shall take fire from the others.

In Ralph's camp on the beach, Piggy gives Ralph his glasses to start the fire. They wish that they could make a radio or a boat, but Ralph says that if they do so, they risk being captured by the Reds. Eric stops himself before he can admit that it would be better than being captured by Jack's hunters. Ralph wonders what Simon had been saying about a dead man. The boys become tired from pulling wood for the fire, but Ralph insists that they must keep it going. Ralph nearly forgets what their objective is for the fire, and they then realize that two people are needed to keep the fire burning at all times. Given their small numbers, each member of Ralph's group would have to spend twelve hours a day devoted to tending the fire. Exhausted and discouraged, they give up the fire for the night and return to the shelters, where they drift off to sleep.

Ralph and Piggy sleep fitfully. They are wakened by sounds within the shelter: Samneric play-fighting. Aware of his increasing fear, Ralph reminisces about the safety of home, and he and Piggy conclude that they will go insane. Suddenly, they hear the leaves rustling outside their shelter and a boy's voice whispering Piggy's name. It is Jack with his hunters, who are attacking the shelter. Ralph's boys fight them off but suffer considerable injuries. Piggy tells Ralph that they wanted the conch, but he then realizes that they came for something else: Piggy's broken glasses.

Analysis

As the chaos surrounding Simon's death calms down, Golding focuses on the horror Piggy and Ralph feel about their involvement in the murder. The two boys attempt to justify their role in Simon's death with the ideas that they did not know that it was Simon until it was too late, they were not among the inner circle of boys beating him to death, and they operated on instinct rather than on malice. Still, the involvement of Piggy and Ralph makes clear that even these two, the paragons of rationality and maturity among the children on the island, are susceptible to the same forces that motivate Jack and his hunters. Golding obscures the once-clear dichotomy between the "good" Ralph and the "evil" Jack, demonstrating that the compulsion towards violence and destruction is present inside all individuals. The reverse, a "good" Jack, is rarely in evidence. The implication of Ralph's and Piggy's brief but tragic participation in the brutal activities of Jack's tribe is that the natural state of humanity is neither good nor evil but mixed. Social order and rules, with conscience and reason helping out only on occasion, are what constrain and limit the "evil" impulses that exist inside us all.

Indeed, Golding does present one major qualification that distinguishes Ralph and Piggy from Jack. Ralph and Piggy still possess a moral sensibility. They realize that their actions are wrong and accordingly struggle to find some justification for their parts in the murder. They are ashamed of the murder, unlike the other boys, who show no qualms about what they have done. Even if Ralph and Piggy present unsuccessful rationalizations, the fact that they need to find some reason for their behavior shows that they have an understanding of moral principles and retain an appreciation for them. Golding thus suggests that while evil may be present inside all of us, the strength of conscience and reason can positively move one's morals, for some more than for others.

As the new leader of the boys, Jack maintains his authority by capitalizing on the fears and suspicions of the others. Even when presented with information that the figure on the mountain is not harmful, Jack continues to promote fear of the dreaded beast. Like many tyrants, his rules are based on a strict distinction between insiders and outsiders: the insiders are his tribe, and the outsiders are their common enemies: the beast and the boys on the island who reject Jack's authority. His methods of rule are entirely exclusionary, and they fail to provide that first role of government, the

security and the safety of the group, even while Jack purports to be able to provide protection from the beast and other enemies. The formal declaration by the guard that visitors must announce their presence does nothing to improve the boys' safety.

Even as Golding continues to emphasize the successful rise of Jack as a leader, he suggests that this rule may be short-lived. The shortsightedness Jack displays as a ruler is clear even to Jack himself. Intent on pleasing the boys with games and hunting, he does nothing to address more practical concerns. Faced with the dilemma of providing a feast without a fire, his solution is to steal from the boys who have maintained a sense of responsibility. Ralph, Piggy, Sam and Eric are therefore considerably burdened. Without help from the other boys who are content to play as savages, these four must devote all their energy to maintaining the signal fire, an almost impossible task. The strain Jack has left the boys with is considerable, but this does not matter to Jack if he can only secure the glasses for fire for the feasts. Ralph and Piggy muse, for their part, that they may go insane if they are not rescued soon.

A more immediate danger to Ralph and Piggy comes when Jack and his followers charge the camp on the beach. The attack on Ralph and Piggy signals yet another stage in the boys' descent from civilized behavior into pure savagery. The murder of Simon was motivated by mass hysteria, instinctual fear, and panic. Here the violence used to gain Piggy's glasses, even though it is not fatal, is intentional, an act that anticipates the murder of Piggy in the following chapter. Piggy's premeditated murder is also foreshadowed by the description of the rock perched near the fortress. Jack and his soldiers have placed the rock so that it may be tipped over on another boy. The question remains regarding which boy will suffer this fate.

As in previous chapters, Golding uses symbolism and imagery to call the reader's attention to the novel's tragic arc, which follows the boys as they devolve from civilized, moral human beings to animal-like savages, motivated only by self-interest and given over to violent impulse. Piggy's glasses, throughout the novel a symbol of intellectual reason and pragmatism-they are used to start the signal fire-come into the hands of the irrational and brutal Jack. Jack, of course, wants the glasses to start not a signal fire, but a bonfire for a pig roast, a decision that reflects his shortsightedness and hedonism. We may also notice that Ralph and Piggy are surprised by the theft of the glasses, since they thought Jack's intent was to steal the conch shell. Jack's disinterest in the conch, a symbol in the novel for democratic authority, reflects his rejection not only of Ralph's authority, but also of the entire system of liberal democracy. The conch is useless if one does not believe in its power. Ralph apparently still thinks that the conch matters or should matter. The image of Ralph clutching the conch is a powerful reminder that he is one of only a few boys who still believe in civilized life on the island.

As the conch shell is divested of meaning and Piggy's glasses fall into the hands of Jack's tribe, Ralph and Piggy become desolate and depressed, hopeless that they will ever be rescued. Golding emphasizes the despair of Ralph's group to provoke pessimism in the reader. That is, when Ralph and Piggy no longer have faith in their rescue, we lose hope for them as well. Rather, it appears that the boys' future will forever be on and of the island, guided by the demented but flourishing tribal system of Jack and his hunters. The scene on Ralph's beach, with its declining and injured population, dwindling fire, and meaningless cultural symbols (in particular the conch) stands in sharp contrast to the scene in Jack's forest, with its army, enforced borders, and even weaponry (the defense contraption). The implication is less that Ralph's civilization has been destroyed than that it has been replaced by another, more primitive but more warlike society. As the boys' early days on the island mirrored the evolutionary progress of early man, the boys' final days mirror some aspects of the development of human civilizations, which clash violently over religious and political differences.

Summary and Analysis of Chapter Eleven: Castle Rock

On the beach Ralph, Piggy, and Samneric gather around the remains of the signal fire, bloody and wounded. They attempt to rekindle the fire, but it is impossible without Piggy's glasses. Ralph, blowing the conch, calls an assembly of the boys who remain with them. Piggy, squinting and unable to see, asks Ralph to instruct them about what can be done. Ralph responds that what they most need is a fire, and he reminds them that if they had kept the fire burning they might have been rescued already. Realizing the importance of Piggy's glasses, Ralph, Sam, and Eric think that they should go to the Castle Rock with spears, but Piggy refuses to arm himself. Piggy says that he is going to go find Jack himself and appeal to his sense of justice. A tear falls down his cheek as he speaks. Ralph says that they should make themselves look presentable, with clothes, to resemble boys and not savages.

Ralph and his boys set off along the beach, limping. When they approach the Castle Rock, Ralph blows the conch, which he has brought with him, believing it will remind Jack and his hunters of his rightful authority. He spots Jack's boys guarding their camp, and he approaches them tentatively. Samneric rush to Ralph's side, leaving Piggy alone. Jack's hunters, unimpressed by the conch shell, throw rocks at Ralph and his companions and shout for them to leave. Suddenly, Jack emerges from the forest, accompanied by a group of hunters who are dragging a dead pig. He warns Ralph to leave them alone. Ralph demands the return of Piggy's glasses, and the two argue. Ralph finally calls Jack a thief, and Jack responds by trying to stab Ralph with his spear, which Ralph deflects.

As Ralph and Jack fight, Piggy reminds Ralph what they came to do. Ralph breaks away from the fight and tells Jack's tribe that they have to give back Piggy's glasses, because they are necessary to maintain the signal fire on the beach. He reminds them that the fire is their only hope for rescue. Frustrated by their indifference to his pleas, Ralph breaks down and calls them painted fools. Jack orders the boys to grab Samneric. The hunters wrestle Samneric's spears from their hands, and Jack orders them to tie up the twins. Ralph again screams at Jack, calling him a beast and a swine and a thief. As they fight again, Piggy, yelling over the boys' jeers, demands that he address the group.

Struggling to be heard over the commotion, Piggy asks the other boys whether it is better to be a pack of painted Indians or to be sensible like Ralph. He asks if they would rather have rules and peaceful agreement or be able only to hunt and kill. He reminds them of the importance of Ralph's rules, which are there to ensure their rescue. Above on the mountain, a frenzied Roger deliberately leans his weight on the log that Robert showed him earlier, dislodging a great rock, which begins to roll down the mountainside. Ralph hears the rock falling and manages to dodge it, but Piggy can neither see nor hear its tumble. The rock crashes down on Piggy, crushing the conch shell, which he was holding, on the way. The rock pushes Piggy down a cliff, where he lands on the beach, dead.

The group falls into a sudden and deep silence. Just as suddenly, however, Jack leaps out of the group, screaming deliriously. He shouts at Ralph that "that's what you'll get" for challenging his authority, and he expresses happiness that the conch is gone. Declaring himself chief, Jack deliberately hurls his spear at Ralph. The spear tears the skin and flesh over Ralph's ribs, then shears off and falls into the water. A terrified Ralph turns and runs, spears now coming at him from different directions. He is propelled by an instinct he never knew he possessed. In his flight, he catches sight of the headless sow from the earlier hunt. After Ralph departs, Jack casts his gaze on the bound Samneric. He orders them to join the tribe, but when they request only to be released, he bullies them, poking the twins in the ribs with a spear. The other boys cheer him on but fall silent when they notice Roger edging past Jack to confront the twins.

Analysis

As the tension between Ralph and Jack comes to a violent head, Golding again establishes the conflict between the two boys as an explicit struggle between savagery and civilization. The two continue to clash over previously developed points of conflict: Ralph criticizes Jack for his lack of responsibility and his ambivalence toward rules of order and justice, and Jack continues to blame Ralph for his lack of direct action against the beast. Their accusations express and emphasize their respective visions of human society on the island: while Ralph is oriented towards a cooperative community organized around the common goal of getting rescued, Jack adheres to a militaristic ideal and unites his tribe around a shared interest in hunting, self-gratification, and fear of the mythical island beast.

Unfortunately, Ralph's criticisms fall on deaf ears, for they are based on the assumption that Jack and his hunters are members of a society with moral codes and regulations. Ralph is appealing to standards Jack no longer believes in, as is symbolized by his glee when the conch shell is crushed. The shift in the struggle between Ralph and Jack is subtle but significant. Previously Jack and Ralph debated over the type of civilization that should predominate on the island: the former advocated a militaristic culture and the latter a liberal community. Now, with Jack's repudiation of any rational system, the two now argue over whether there should be any ordered society at all on the island. One might think of Jack as Plato's Callicles from the Gorgias or Plato's Thrasymachus from the Republic.

The political subtext of the chapter is most evident, however, in the final confrontation between Ralph, Piggy, and Jack. As Ralph and Piggy face Jack and the other boys, Golding clearly delineates the tension between civilization and animalistic savagery. Before they face Jack, Ralph and Piggy deliberately readopt the manners and customs of English society, grooming themselves and dressing themselves as proper English boys. They do so to exaggerate their differences from the hunters, who wear little if any clothing and who adorn themselves with "native" makeup. When Piggy speaks to the boys, he explicitly expresses the major question the novel explores, asking whether it is better to live sensibly according to rules and standards of behavior or to live in a state of anarchy (again, one might turn to Plato's Republic for guidance on this question and others raised by Piggy and the events of the novel). It is significant that the most insightful, reasoned statement in the novel is the one that provokes the most horrific tragedy on the island: the murder of the rational Piggy by the brutal and amoral Roger.

With his death, Piggy joins Simon as the second martyr among the boys. There are several parallels between their respective murders. The two outcasts both die when they shatter the illusions held by the other boys. Simon dies when he exposes the truth about the nonexistent beast, while the hunters kill Piggy when he forces them to see their behavior as barbaric and irresponsible. The murder of Piggy, however, is a more chilling event, for the boys killed Simon out of an instinctual panic. In contrast to the frenzied hunters, Roger has a clear understanding of his actions when he tips the rock that kills Piggy. This event thus completes the progression of behavior that Golding developed in the previous two chapters: the boys have moved from unintentional violence to completely premeditated murder. The chapter's final image, in which Piggy's murderer, Roger, edges past Jack to approach the bound twins, implies that Roger's brutality surpasses even Jack's. While Jack condones and participates in violence against animals and humans alike, it is Roger who orchestrates and carries out the murder of Piggy. Significantly, he does not seek authorization from Jack for the murder or for the implied torture of Samneric. Rather, his sadism appears to be entirely self-interested, and it suggests that he is a potential threat to Jack's authority.

The novel's major symbol of civilization, the conch shell, appears in this chapter only to be destroyed after Roger pushes the boulder onto Piggy. This crucial act provokes and foreshadows Ralph's destruction of the Lord of the Flies, the primary cultural symbol of Jack's tribe, in the next and final chapter of the novel. The gesture will suggest Ralph's own descent into savagery and violence. The conch, an established marker of Ralph's authority and a consistent symbol for liberal democracy throughout the novel, has lost power; Jack and his hunters long ago refused to recognize it as a symbol of authority. In this chapter, the conch is finally destroyed in a demonstration of the triumph of Jack's will over Ralph's.

As Ralph flees from the spears of Jack's hunters, Golding again draws the reader's attention to the lower, immoral, animalistic humanity that lurks inside every individual. Ralph is literally being hunted like the pigs on the island, a moment that was foreshadowed in previous chapters when Roger pretended to be a pig in the hunting dance, and when Jack suggested to the group that they should hunt a littlun. Boy and animal become indistinct, and as Ralph flees he is propelled by a primitive subhuman instinct. His terror is that of a hunted animal: instinctual, unthinking, and primal. Ralph, the character who throughout the novel stood for pragmatism and civilization, has been reduced to an animal of prey, just as Jack and his hunters have reduced themselves to predatory beasts. (For more on the theme of humans and animals, compare The Island of Dr. Moreau by H. G. Wells.)

Note also the presence of animals in this penultimate chapter. Throughout the novel, Golding has used animal imagery and metaphors to call the reader's attention to the delicate line between human and animal nature, as well as to highlight the hostile relationship between civilization and the natural world that civilization subdues in order to ensure human survival. As Ralph flees the spears of Jack and his hunters, the last thing he registers is the headless body of the sow that Jack's tribe had just slaughtered. The image of the sow's body evokes both the Lord of the Flies, a pig's head on a stick that has signified evil, and Piggy, whose brutal murder marks the final destruction of civilization on the island.

Summary and Analysis of Chapter Twelve: Cry of the Hunters

Ralph hides in the jungle, worrying about his wounds and the inhuman violence into which the boys on the island have devolved. He thinks about Simon and Piggy and realizes that civilization is now impossible among the boys. Ralph, who is not far from the Castle Rock, thinks he sees Bill in the distance. He concludes that the boy is not Bill-at least not any more. This boy is a savage, entirely different from the boy in shorts and shirt he once knew. Ralph is certain that Jack will never leave him alone. Noticing the Lord of the Flies, now just a skull with the skin and meat eaten away, Ralph decides to fight back. He knocks the skull from the stick, which he takes, intending to use it as a spear. From a distance, Ralph can still make out the boys' chant: "Kill the beast. Cut his throat. Spill his blood."

That night, armed with his makeshift spear, Ralph crawls undetected to the lookout near Castle Rock. He calls to Sam and Eric, who are now guarding the entrance. Sam gives Ralph a chunk of meat but does not agree to join him again. Sam tells Ralph to leave. The twins tell Ralph that Roger has sharpened a stick at both ends, and they warn him that Jack will be sending the entire tribe after Ralph the following day. Dejected, Ralph crawls away to a thicket where he can safely sleep. When he awakes in the morning, he can hear Jack torturing one of the twins and talking to Roger outside the thicket where he hides. They are trying to find out where Ralph is hiding. Several other boys are rolling rocks down the mountain, trying to break into the thicket. More boys are trying to climb in.

Just as Ralph decides to find a new hiding place, he smells smoke. He realizes with horror that Jack has set the forest on fire in an attempt to smoke Ralph out of hiding. He also recognizes that the fire will destroy all the fruit on the island, again endangering the boys' basic survival. Terrified, Ralph bolts from his hiding place, fighting his way past several of Jack's hunters, who are painted in wild colors and carrying sharpened wooden spears. Wielding their spears menacingly, they chase Ralph through the forest. Weaving through the dense underbrush, Ralph finally escapes to the beach, where he collapses in exhaustion and terror. He is aware that Jack's hunters are close behind.

When Ralph looks up, he is surprised to see a figure looming over him. He realizes that the figure is a man-a naval officer! The officer tells Ralph that his ship saw the smoke and decided to investigate the island. Ralph realizes that the officer is under the impression that the boys have been only playing games. The other boys begin to appear from the forest, and the officer begins to realize the chaos and violence among the stranded boys. Percival tries to tell him his name and address but finds he can no longer remember it. Ralph, informing him that he is boss, is sad to find he cannot answer the officer when asked how many boys are on the island. The officer, aware that they have not been behaving according to the rules of civilization, scolds the boys for not knowing exactly how many they are and for not being organized, as the British are supposed to be.

Ralph insists to the officer that they were organized and good at first. The officer says he imagines it was like the "show" in *The Coral Island*. Ralph, not understanding his reference, begins to weep for the early days on the island, which now seem impossibly remote. He weeps for the end of innocence and the darkness of man's heart, and he weeps for the deaths of Simon and Piggy. All of the other boys begin to cry as well. The officer turns away, embarrassed, while the other boys attempt to regain their composure. The officer keeps his eye on the cruiser in the distance.

Analysis

The dynamic of interaction between Ralph and the other boys changes dramatically in the opening scenes of the final chapter. Ralph is now an object to the other boys as he flees Jack's hunters, who seem unable to make the distinction between hunting pigs and hunting each other. As Ralph observes, the other boys on the island bear no resemblance to the English schoolboys first stranded there; they are complete savages without either moral or rational sensibilities. As they cease to exhibit the qualities that define them as civilized human beings, they no longer qualify as boys. This shift from human to animal identity is noticeable now in Ralph. No longer considered human by the other boys, he must rely on his primitive senses to escape the hunters. Because Ralph can no longer defend himself through any sense of justice or morality, he must use his animal instinct and cunning to survive.

The final chapter emphasizes the self-destructive quality of the boys' actions. Throughout the novel, Golding has indicated that the boys are destructive not only to their enemies, but to themselves, a theme that culminates dramatically in this chapter. Images of decay permeate the final scenes, particularly in the Lord of the Flies, which decayed until it became only a hollow skull. Significantly, Ralph dismantles the Lord of the Flies by pushing the pig's skull off of the stick it was impaled on, an act that mirrors and completes Roger's destruction of the conch in the previous chapter. The destruction of both objects signals to the reader that the boys have been plunged into a brutal civil war. Ralph takes apart the Lord of the Flies-a totem for Jack's tribe-to use the stick it is impaled on as a spear with which to attack Jack. Ralph's action thus indicates that he has accepted Jack's savage terms of war, a conflict he had previously approached with reason and nonviolence, but it is too late for that. Ralph's decision to attack Jack or at least to defend himself with a weapon indicates that he too has devolved into savagery. All vestiges of democratic civilization on the island are gone, and it is unclear if Jack's monarchy retains any civilization at all.

Another ominous image in this chapter is Roger's spear. As Samneric inform Ralph, Roger has sharpened a spear at both ends, a tool that symbolizes the danger the boys have created for themselves. The spear simultaneously points at the one who wields it and the one at whom it is directed; it is capable of harming both equally. The significance of the double-edged spear is demonstrated in the boys' hunt for Ralph. That is, in order to find Ralph, the boys start a fire that might overwhelm them and destroy the fruit that is essential for their survival. Golding thus alerts the reader to the counterproductive consequences of vengeance: in the world of the novel, the ultimate price of harming another is harming oneself.

Despite the seemingly hopeless situation on the island, however, the boys are finally rescued by a naval officer whose ship noticed the fire on the island. This ending is not only unexpected but deeply ironic. It was not the signal fire that attracted the navy cruiser. Instead it was the forest fire that Jack's tribe set in an extreme gesture of irresponsibility and self-destruction. Ironically and even tragically, it is Jack and not Ralph who is ultimately responsible for the boys' rescue. The implications are grim: it was not careful planning and foresight that brought the boys to safety, but a coincidence. The consequences of savagery, not civilization, are what saved the children. With this abrupt narrative gesture, Golding overturns the logic he had established throughout the novel. Of course, poetic justice is not required, but the issue is vexing. Perhaps, he suggests, savagery and civilization are less unlike than we believe. By casting Jack as the boys' unintentional savior, Golding ends the novel before the action can properly climax. The reader is denied a chance to see a final battle between Ralph and Jack, although we can easily imagine that Ralph is doomed. Since the dehumanization is complete, there is almost nothing more to be said.

The sudden appearance of the naval officer at the beach mitigates the effects of the boys' aggression. The officer is a deus ex machina (an unexpected figure who shows up almost out of nowhere and who appears only to wrap up the plot and bring it to a speedy conclusion). His arrival on the island frees Golding from having to explore the final implications of the hunters' suicidal attack on Ralph and Ralph's own descent into violent brutality.

In another unlikely gesture, the naval officer repeats to the boys the lessons that, throughout the novel, Ralph and Piggy had attempted to impart to the other boys. He emphasizes the importance of order just as Ralph and Piggy had, thus retroactively calling attention to the maturity and sensibility of Ralph's advice to the other boys. Nevertheless, the naval officer cannot comprehend the full reach of the boys' experience on the island. He interprets the hunting and painted faces as a childish game, unaware that their dress carries more than symbolic meaning. The boys have not been playing as savages; they have become them. The officer's mention of the nineteenth-century adventure novel *The Coral Island* underscores his ignorance of the brutality that is dominating the island. While the boys in *The Coral Island* had carefree, childish adventures, the boys in Golding's narrative actually descended into unthinkable depths of violence and cruelty. Through the officer's naivete as informed by *The Coral Island*, Golding again implicitly critiques the idealistic portrayals of children in popular literature. Still, these unlikely concluding events feel abrupt and unsatisfying after so much richness in the narrative.

Another significant aspect of the naval officer's character is his admonition to the boys that they are not behaving like proper "British boys," which recalls Jack's patriotic claims in Chapter Two that the British are the best at everything. The officer's statement symbolically links him to Jack and underscores the hypocrisy of such a military character. While the officer condemns the violent play of the boys on the island, he is himself a military figure, engaged in an ongoing war that itself necessitated the boys' evacuation from their homeland and (unintentionally) led to the events on the island. Again, the issue is ambiguous: perhaps the violence among the boys was not an expression of an unrestrained inner instinct but a reflection of the seemingly "civilized" culture they were raised in, a culture engaged in an ugly and fatal war. In any case, the officer echoes Ralph rather than Jack, repeating many of the warnings about rules and order that Ralph had expressed to the boys throughout the novel. By associating the officer with both Ralph and Jack, in different ways, Golding calls into question the distinction between civilization and savagery that he traced with increasing emphasis in the novel's earlier chapters and then erased in later chapters.

If the naval officer saves the boys from their self-destruction, he may have come too late. The final scenes of the novel emphasize the permanent emotional damage that the boys have inflicted on themselves. With the possible exception of Ralph, the boys are no longer accustomed to the society from which they came. Golding underscores this fact by presenting Percival as unable to state his name and address as he could when the boys first arrived on the island. More importantly, Ralph perceives their experiences on the island as the end of their innocence. He has witnessed the overthrow of rational society as represented by Piggy in favor of the barbarism and tyranny of Jack. His final thoughts: "Ralph wept for the end of innocence, the darkness of man's heart, and the fall through the air of the true, wise friend called Piggy." These thoughts indicate a play of the Eden myth with which Golding began. If there was an Eden on the island, it was the special place found by Simon that none of the other boys wanted to experience. They began out of Eden rather than inside it. Any paradise they hoped for on the island came to an end when the boys chose nature and instinct over rationality and awareness-compare, however, the rise of rationality and awareness in Genesis, which seems to occur most of all *after* the Fall. Ralph loses his innocence when he realizes that the violence inherent in humanity is always under the surface of the order and morality that civilization imposes on individuals.

Suggested Essay Questions

1. In his introduction to William Golding's novel, novelist E.M. Forster suggests that Golding's writing "lays a solid foundation for the horrors to come." Using Forster's quote as a starting point, discuss how the novel foreshadows the murders of Simon and Piggy. Focus on two events or images from the novel's earlier chapters and describe how they anticipate the novel's tragic outcome.

   Answer: The weather on the island grows increasingly more hostile and ominous as the novel's plot unfolds, Piggy's name suggests that he will be killed like an animal, and so on.

2. Many critics have read Lord of the Flies as a political allegory. In particular, they have considered the novel a commentary on the essential opposition between totalitarianism and liberal democracy. Using two or three concrete examples from the novel, show how the two political ideologies are figured in the novel, and then discuss which of the two you think Golding seems to favor.

   Answer: The contrast between Ralph's group on the beach and Jack's tribe at Castle Rock represents the opposition between liberal democracy and totalitarianism. Golding presents the former as the superior system, demonstrated by the success of the assembly among Jack's group of boys and the ordered system that prioritizes the ongoing signal fire on the mountain, tactics that ensure the welfare of the entire group. Note, though, what happens in both groups over time.

3. Names and naming are important in Lord of the Flies. Many characters have names that allude to other works of literature, give insight into their character, or foreshadow key events. Discuss the significance of the names of, for instance, Sam and Eric, Piggy, and Simon. What does the character's name say about him and his significance? Use external sources as necessary.

   Answer: Piggy's name, for example, indicates his inferior position within the social hierarchy of the island and foreshadows his eventual death at the hands of Jack's tribe. Simon was the name of Peter in the Bible. Jack might be named after John Marcher in Henry James's story *The Beast in the Jungle*, and so on.

4. Two major symbols in the novel are the conch shell and The Lord of the Flies (the pig's head on a stick). Analyze one or both of these symbols in terms of how they are perceived by the boys as well as what they symbolize for the reader.

   Answer: The conch shell represents liberal democracy and order, as endorsed by Ralph and Piggy. The Lord of the Flies tends to represent an autocratic or a primitive order. Note the "exchange" of these objects at the novel's conclusion when the conch is smashed in Jack's camp and Ralph uses part of the Lord of the Flies as a weapon.

5. The children stranded on the island are all boys, and female characters are rarely discussed. How does this matter for the novel?

Answer: Gender difference is not explicitly discussed or represented in the novel, although femininity is symbolically present in the novel's representations of nature. Some of the male characters are "feminized" by the other boys when they are considered un-masculine or vulnerable. In a boys' choir, many boys have high voices that can sing parts normally reserved for females. It is unclear whether Jack's tribe would have become so violent (and nearly naked) if girls of the same age were on the island.

6. At the end of Chapter Eleven, Roger pushes Jack aside to descend on the bound twins "as one who wielded a nameless authority." Focusing on this quotation, discuss Roger's actions in Chapter Eleven in relation to Jack's power and political system.

Answer: Roger's actions towards the twins are unauthorized by Jack, indicating that Jack's own authority is under threat. Golding hints at a shift in the power system among Jack's tribe, which highlights the inherent flaws in Jack's system of military dictatorship.

7. Jack gains power over many of the boys by exploiting their fear of the mythical beast. How does Jack manipulate the myth of the beast to legitimize his authority?

Answer: Jack exploits the boys' fear of the beast to usurp leadership from Ralph, who stresses a rational approach to the presumed evil presence on the island. Within Jack's tribe, the beast continues to have a powerful symbolic and political significance among the boys, uniting them and ensuring their loyalty to Jack's leadership. When Jack first attempts to break away from Ralph's tribe, his authority is not recognized, but as the boys' fear of the beast increases, an increasing number defect from Ralph's group to Jack's, where the existence of the beast is not only acknowledged but is a central fact of day-to-day life.

8. By Chapter Three, the boys are divided into two groups: the older boys and the younger boys or "littluns." What role do the littluns have to play?

Answer: Consider especially the distinction between savagery and civilization.

What happens with the "littluns" registers the increasing brutality on the island. The earliest examples of violence in the novel are directed against the littluns, acts that foreshadow the violent events of later chapters. Moreover, characters who are kind to the littluns tend to remain most closely associated with civilization throughout the novel.

9. The novel's narrative action draws an increasingly firm line between savagery and civilization, yet the value of each becomes an issue in the conclusion, when Jack's fire saves the boys. Using these terms, what is the novel suggesting about human nature, evil, and human civilization?

Answer: The naval officer is a military figure, which reminds the reader that "civilized" societies also engage in violence and murder. Evil seems to be a force that threatens human nature and human civilization--from within. Still, evil is associated primarily with savagery and the worse part of our natures.

10. How does the novel reflect the Cold War and the public's concerns about the conflict between democracy and communism? Does the novel take a side? (Remember to cite all of your research sources in your bibliography.)

Answer: The Cold War was primarily between the democratic U.S. and its allies on the one hand, and the communist U.S.S.R. and its allies on the other hand. The initial events of the novel, following a group of boys in the aftermath of a terrible nuclear war, reflect and capitalize on widespread anxiety about the arms race for destructive atomic weapons. Ralph comes to represent the West and its values, while Jack comes to represent the enemy.

Suggested Essay Questions

The Lord of the Flies: Biblical Allegory or Anti-Religious Critique?

One of the major points of debate between critics who have studied Lord of the Flies is the significance of the substantial number of allusions to Judeo-Christian mythology. While many scholars have argued that these references qualify the novel as biblical allegory, others have suggested that the novel's allusions to the Old and New Testaments turn out to be ironic and thus criticize religion. A careful reading of Lord of the Flies should take into account not only the abundance of biblical images and themes in the text, but also the ways in which religion and religious themes are used.

In particular, the biblical account of good and evil is invoked-but the account in the novel is not quite the same. Take, for instance, the narrative of Eden. The early chapters of the novel, the island itself resembles the Garden of Eden from Genesis, with its picturesque scenery, abundant fruit, and idyllic weather. Accordingly, the boys are symbolically linked to Adam and Eve before the fall. Ralph's first act after the plane crash is to remove his clothes and bathe in the water, a gesture that recalls the nudity of the innocent Adam and Eve and the act of baptism, a Christian rite which, by some accounts, renews in the sinner a state of grace. Naming also becomes important in Genesis, reflected in the novel as the boys give their names. Golding extends the Edenic allusion when he presents the contentment of island life as soon corrupted by fear, a moment that is first signified by reports of a creature the boys refer to as "snake-thing." The "snake-thing" recalls the presence of Satan in the Garden of Eden, who disguised himself as a serpent. But unlike Adam and Eve, the boys are mistaken about the creature, which is not a force external (like Satan) but a projection of the evil impulses that are innate within themselves and the human psyche. Still, it is the boys' failure to recognize the danger of the evil within themselves that propels them deeply into a state of savagery and violence. They continue to externalize it as a beast (again "Lord of the Flies" and "the Beast" are used in religion to refer to Satan), but they become more and more irrational in their perception of it, and they end up developing alternative religious ideas about the Beast and what it wants and does. Although Satan in the Genesis account also has been read as a reflection of evil within human nature, readers usually consider Satan an external force. Original sin enters human nature because of Satan. Without a real Satan in the novel, however, Golding stresses the ways that this Eden is already fallen; for these boys, evil already is within them waiting to be discovered.

On the positive side, Simon's story is that of a prophet or of Jesus Christ. Simon is deeply spiritual, compassionate, non-violent, and in harmony with the natural world. Like many biblical prophets and like Jesus, he is ostracized and ridiculed as an "outsider" for what the others perceive as his "queer" or unorthodox behavior. Critics also have noted that Simon's confrontation with The Lord of the Flies resembles Christ's conversation with the devil during his forty days in the wilderness as described in the New Testament gospels, and critics have noted parallels between

Simon's murder and Christ's sacrifice on the cross. But Simon's revelation is more of a debunking and a turn to the secular, rather than a prophetic condemnation of evil or a call to the higher things. His revelation is that the beast does not exist but is just a dead human.

Author of ClassicNote and Sources

Jeremy Ross, author of ClassicNote. Completed on April 14, 2000, copyright held by GradeSaver.

Updated and revised A. Kimball, December 8, 2006, and A. Kissel, August 18, 2007. Copyright held by GradeSaver.

Baker, James R. William Golding. New York: St. Martin's Press, 1965.

Bloom, Harold, ed. Lord of the Flies: Modern Critical Interpretations. New York: Chelsea House, 1998.

Golding, William. Lord of the Flies. New York: Coward, McCann & Geoghegan, Inc., 1954.

Olsen, Kirsten. Understanding The Lord of the Flies: A Student Casebook to Issues, Sources and Historical Documents. New York: Greenwood Publishing Group, 2000.

Swisher, Clarice, ed. Readings on The Lord of the Flies. New York: Greenhaven Press, 1997.

Forster, E.M. "Introduction." Lord of the Flies. New York: Coward, McCann & Geoghegan Inc., 1962. ix-xiii.

Essay: Two Faces of Man

by Anonymous
April 14, 2000

William Golding was inspired by his experiences in the Royal Navy during World War II when he wrote Lord of the Flies (Beetz 2514). Golding has said this about his book:

> The theme is an attempt to trace the defeats of society back to the defects of human nature. The moral is that the shape of society must depend on the ethical nature of the individual and not on any political system however apparently logical or respectable. The whole book is symbolic in nature except the rescue in the end where adult life appears, dignified and capable, but in reality enmeshed in the same evil as the symbolic life of the children on the island. (Epstein 204)

In the novel he displays the two different personalities that mankind possesses, one civilized, the other primitive. Golding uses the setting, characters, and symbolism in Lord of the Flies to give the reader a detailed description of these two faces of man.

The story's setting is essential for the evolution of both sides of man. When an airplane carrying a bunch of school boys crashes on an island, only the children survive. The island the children find themselves on is roughly boat-shaped (Golding 29; ch. 1). It is ironic that the children are stuck on an island shaped like the thing that could save them (a boat). Despite this irony, they are trapped. They are surrounded by ocean and no one knows where they are. The boys, isolated from society, must now create their own.

The children soon realize that there are, "No grownups!" (Golding 8; ch. 1) This means that the boys must fend for themselves until they are rescued. There are no parents or adults to give the boys rules or punish them if they do wrong, so they must learn how to control and govern themselves. Their first attempt mimics the society that they have grown up with, that of a civilized democracy (Michel-Michot 175). A conch shell is used to call assemblies and decisions are voted on (Golding 17, ch. 1). The fire that they try to keep going on the top of the mountain is a symbol of their civilized society because it represents their hopes for rescue and a return to their ordinary lives (Michel-Michot 175).

Unfortunately, the children soon grow tired of this civilized life. They want to have fun and quickly lose interest in whatever job they are doing. Ralph states the problem when he says to the group of children, " We have lots of assemblies. Everybody enjoys speaking and being together. We decide things. But they don't get done. We were going to have water brought from the stream and left in those coconut shells under fresh leaves. So it was for a few days. Now there's no water. The shells are dry. People drink from the river.' " (Golding 79; ch. 5) All of their resolutions soon degrade and fall apart. The society gives into its more primitive side and now only concerns itself with having fun. Hunting, which originally was only a practice of getting food so that they could survive until they were rescued becomes all important. (Michel-Michot 175-6) All of the children's fears become condensed into a monster that they fear and awe. They make sacrifices to "the beast" to appease it and keep themselves safe (Golding 137; ch. 8). In the end, their grand society becomes no better than a bunch of savages in this lush island setting.

The island is abundant in resources, with lots of fresh water and plentiful fruit ripe for the picking. "He walked with an accustomed tread through the acres of fruit trees, where the least energetic could find an easy if unsatisfying meal." (Golding 56; ch. 3) Although rich with nature's splendor, the children are sorely lacking in the technology with which they have become accustomed to. They do not even have matches. If not for Piggy's "specs", they would not be able to create fire (Golding 42; ch. 2). This lack of technology both hinders their attempts to be civilized and hastens their progression towards savagery.

The story's characters serve as archetypes that display the struggle between man's quest for civilization and his urges to become primitive. The most important characters in the story are Ralph, Piggy, Simon, and Jack. Roger, Sam, and Eric, although not as important as the others, also serve to add color to the story and lend to its progression towards savagery.

Ralph is the story's protagonist. He is a natural leader because of his superior height, strength, and good looks (Rosenfield 172). He is also the democratic man, the keeper of the civilized ways (Spitz 173). He was chosen chief by a vote from his peers and strives to maintain order, to "rule through persuasion, with the consent of the governed." (Spitz 173) Ralph is "every man" and his body serves as the battle ground between reason and instinct. (Rosenfield 172)

Ralph loses this battle and eventually starts to regress to a primitive state. This is shown near the end of the story when he has trouble reasoning things through. "Then, at the moment of greatest passion and conviction, that curtain flapped in his head and he forgot what he had been driving at." (Golding 163; ch. 10) Ralph's regression continues until he is no more than an animal, who uses its most basic instincts to escape the fire which threatens to burn the island down and the rest of the tribe who want to hunt him down (Babb 11). "He [Ralph] shot forward, burst the thicket, was in the open, screaming, snarling, bloody." (Golding 199; ch. 12)

Piggy is fat, nearly blind, and asthmatic. He also embodies reason and intelligence. Piggy represents rationality, logic, science, and the ways of thinking that a civilized society depends on (Taylor 170). He has a strong urge to distinguish and to order until reduced to a manageable system (Magill 826). He insists on collecting the names of all the stranded children, using the conch to call assemblies, and having

Essay: Two Faces of Man

meetings (Babb 11).

Piggy is the brains behind Ralph's leadership. Piggy is the first one who suggests using the conch Ralph found to assemble the others (Golding 17; ch. 1). He is the one who brings Ralph back to the topic at hand near the end of the novel when Ralph's reasoning starts to deteriorate under the constant pressure of trying to remain civilized (Babb 22). He assumes that civilized society is all powerful because it seems more reasonable for people to co-exist with rules and mutual respect, rather than obedience and terror (Beetz 2515). " Which is better- to have rules and agree, or to hunt and kill?' " (Golding 180; ch. 11)

Simon is the Christ figure of the book and the voice of revelation (Spitz 172). He consistently reveals a kindness that no one else seems to possess whether it be through his comforting of Ralph, offering of food to Piggy , or getting fruits for the younger children (Babb 24). He is the most self-conscious of the boys, and prefers to withdraw into solitude for lonely mediations (Magill 827). He is the first to suggest that there is no beast, that, " . . . maybe it's only us.' " (Golding 89; ch. 5). Simon seeks to confront his fears and comes to accept the evil that exists both in him and in everyone (Babb 30-1). He does this by speaking to a pig head that was put on a stick and climbing the mountain to find that the "beast" is really just a dead pilot (Golding 137; ch. 8). Simon is mistaken for the "beast" when he comes back to explain to the rest of the children what he found and is ironically killed by those he wished to save (Golding 152; ch. 9).

Jack is the novel's antagonist. He is the opposite of Ralph, distinguished by his ugliness and red hair (Rosenfield 172). He loses both elections when voting on who will become the leader of the group and is obsessed with power. This is why he is so intent on hunting, it is a way of imposing his will upon a living thing (Babb 9).

Jack's rise to power first begins when the younger children's fears start to distort their surroundings: twigs become creepers, shadows become demons, etc. (Rosenfield 173). Jack uses this fear to become the younger children's protector. If they do what he says, the "beast" cannot get them. Jack soon decides to form his own society. It becomes based on this kind of ceremonial obeisance to himself and is shown by those sacrifices by which the tribe creates its beast, thereby sanctifying the fear and irrationality that govern the children's actions (Babb 21).

Roger is Jack's henchman. He has a sadistic soul and delights in tormenting others. An example of this is when he throws stones at a younger child when nobody is watching (Golding 62; ch. 4). As the children's society degrades, Roger slowly loses the inhibitions that society has imposed upon him. Where once he was afraid to hit a child with a stone when no one was around, he soon becomes a deadly enforcer. He kills Piggy by pushing a bolder on him while in plain sight of everyone and also tortures Sam and Eric until they tell him where Ralph is hiding (Golding 180-1; ch. 11). Roger gladly enacts the evil deeds that help the story progress in its downward spiral towards savagery.

Sam and Eric are identical twins in this novel. In the beginning, they are two separate beings, but as time goes on they merge into one being, "Samneric" (Golding 182; ch. 11). They represent the average man of good who will stick to his principles for as long as possible, but will eventually join the majority when it becomes too hard to stand alone on his own ground (Michel-Michot 177). This is shown by their fierce loyalty to Ralph, even when almost all of the other kids have abandoned Ralph's group for Jack's fun tribe. Only after being tortured do they agree to become part of Jack's tribe (Golding 188; ch. 12).

The symbolism in the story lends a deeper meaning to the chain of events that eventually unfurl. Most of these symbols can be divided into two groups: symbols that represent civilization and order, and symbols that represent chaos and savagery.

The conch used to regulate the assemblies is the symbol of democracy and free speech. Although adequate when used to gather the boys together, it holds little power when confronted with violence and tyranny (Michel-Michot 176). This is shown to us when Roger destroys the conch with the same bolder that kills Piggy, effectively destroying the last remnants of Ralph's civilized society (Golding 181; ch. 11).

The signal fire, and Piggy's glasses (which are used to light the fires), are also symbols of civilization. The signal fire represents rescue, but it is also a distant end that will only be reached at the price of an everyday effort (Michel-Michot 176). Like most things in our society, culture and education to name a few, it is a duty that must be done for no immediate end (Michel-Michot 176). Piggy's glasses serve as a marker for their society's progression into darkness. As Piggy loses his sight, so too, do the boys lose sight of their original goal: rescue (Rosenfield 173). One of the lenses of Piggy's glasses breaks after a fight with Jack. The fight started when Jack let the signal fire die out while a ship was passing, thereby costing them a chance at being rescued (Golding 71; ch. 4).

Golding names the pig head that Jack puts on a stick as a sacrifice for the beast, "Lord of the Flies" (Golding 138; ch. 8). It symbolizes the anarchic, amoral, driving force of Jack's tribe (Epstein 205). Only Simon knows that the reason why the beast cannot be found outside is because the beast lives inside all of us. We all have a little of the Lord of the Flies in us.

The "beast" becomes a sign of the children's unrest (Michel-Michot 175). It goes from being a nightmare in some little boy's dreams in the beginning of the novel to something very real that requires sacrifice if one is to be safe (Golding 37; ch. 2). The beast represents the children's superstitious fears which become so overpowering that it eventually takes control of the situation (Michel-Michot 175).

The mask that Jack wears takes away his self-consciousness by striping him of his individuality. When the rest of the group begins to wear masks, they cease being individuals and become a mob. By destroying their personal identity they lose their

Essay: Two Faces of Man

personal responsibility (Magill 827). "He had even glimpsed one of them, striped brown, black, and red, and had judged that it was Bill. But really, thought Ralph, this was not Bill. This was a savage whose image refused to blend with that ancient picture of a boy in shorts and shirt." (Golding 183; ch. 12) Even to Ralph, who once knew him, Bill has become something completely different once he dons the mask and makeup.

The sequence of killing can be used to track the children's turning from innocence to savagery (Babb 14-5). First, the boy with the birth mark accidentally dies in a fire (Golding 46; ch. 2). Then, Simon dies in a violent act committed by a group of people (Golding 152-3; ch. 9). Piggy is killed by an individual (Roger) quite deliberately (Golding 180-1; ch. 11). Finally the change is complete and the children have become complete savages. They choose to hunt Ralph down near the end of the novel, knowing full well that the hunt will end in murder and sacrifice (Babb 14-5).

William Golding uses Lord of the Flies to teach us that the most dangerous enemy is not the evil found without, but the evil found within each of us. At the end of the novel, Ralph and the other boys realize the horror of their actions:

> The tears began to flow and sobs shook him. He [Ralph] gave himself up to them for the first time on the island; great shuddering spasms of grief that seemed to wrench his whole body. His voice rose under the black smoke before the burning wreckage of the island; and infected by that emotion, the other little boys began to shake and sob too. And in the middle of them, with filthy body, matted hair, and unwiped nose, Ralph wept for the end of innocence . . . (Golding 202; ch. 12).

Unfortunately, the naval officer who rescues them has yet to learn the lesson these boys have. He will take them back to the "civilized" world, which happens to be engulfed in war at the moment. Ironically, the children have survived one primitive and infantile morality system only to be thrown back into a bigger one, World War II (Rosenfield 175). Evil will always be a part of man's nature. Golding's novel was meant to show us that this evil must be accepted, not ignored, or grave will the consequences be.

Works Cited

Golding, William. Lord of the Flies. New York: Berkley, 1954.

Babb, Howard S. The Novels of William Golding. N.p.: Ohio State UP, 1970.

Beetz, Kirk H., ed. Beacham's Encyclopedia of Popular Fiction. Vol. 5. Osprey: n.p., 1996. 5 vols.

Epstein, E. L. Afterword. Lord of the Flies. By William Golding. New York: Berkley, 1954.

Gunton, Sharon R., ed. Contemporary Literary Criticism. Vol. 17. Detroit: Gale, 1981. 68 vols.

Magill, Frank N., ed. Masterplots. Vol. 2. Englewood Cliffs: n.p., 1949. 3 vols.

Matuz, Roger., ed. Contemporary Literary Criticism. Vol. 58. Detroit: Gale, 1990. 68 vols.

Michel-Michot, Paulette. "The Myth of Innocence,". Matuz 175-7.

Rosenfield, Claire. " Men of a Smaller Growth': A Psychological Analysis of William Golding's Lord of the Flies." Matuz 172-5.

Spitz, David. "Power and Authority: An Interpretation of Golding's Lord of the Flies,". Gunton 172-3.

Taylor, Harry H. "The Case against William Golding's Simon-Piggy." Gunton 170-1.

Essay: The Relationship Between Symbolism and Theme in Lord of the Flies

by Anonymous
June 21, 2002

In real life, common objects that are used everyday are often taken for granted and even unusual sights, as well as ideas, are often unrecognized. However, this is seldom the case with similar objects and ideas that literary characters encounter. Many authors use seemingly ordinary, trivial objects in addition to unique elements to symbolize ideas or concepts that help to reveal the theme of their works. In William Golding's Lord of the Flies, the boys who are stranded on the island without supervision come in contact with many such elements. Through the use of symbols such as the beast, the pig's head, and even Piggy's specs, Golding demonstrates that humans, when liberated from society's rules and taboos, allow their natural capacity for evil to dominate their existence.

One of the most important and most obvious symbols in Lord of the Flies is the object that gives the novel its name, the pig's head. Golding's description of the slaughtered animal's head on a spear is very graphic and even frightening. The pig's head is depicted as "dim-eyed, grinning faintly, blood blackening between the teeth," and the "obscene thing" is covered with a "black blob of flies" that "tickled under his nostrils" (William Golding, Lord of the Flies, New York, Putnam Publishing Group, 1954, p. 137, 138). As a result of this detailed, striking image, the reader becomes aware of the great evil and darkness represented by the Lord of the Flies, and when Simon begins to converse with the seemingly inanimate, devil-like object, the source of that wickedness is revealed. Even though the conversation may be entirely a hallucination, Simon learns that the beast, which has long since frightened the other boys on the island, is not an external force. In fact, the head of the slain pig tells him, "Fancy thinking the beast was something you could hunt and kill! Ö You knew, didn't you? I'm part of you?" (p. 143). That is to say, the evil, epitomized by the pig's head, that is causing the boys' island society to decline is that which is inherently present within man. At the end of this scene, the immense evil represented by this powerful symbol can once again be seen as Simon faints after looking into the wide mouth of the pig and seeing "blackness within, a blackness that spread" (p. 144).

Another of the most important symbols used to present the theme of the novel is the beast. In the imaginations of many of the boys, the beast is a tangible source of evil on the island. However, in reality, it represents the evil naturally present within everyone, which is causing life on the island to deteriorate. Simon begins to realize this even before his encounter with the Lord of the Flies, and during one argument over the existence of a beast, he attempts to share his insight with the others. Timidly, Simon tells them, "Maybe, Ö maybe there is a beast Ö What I mean is Ö maybe it's only us" (p. 89). In response to Simon's statement, the other boys, who had once conducted their meetings with some sense of order, immediately begin to argue more fiercely. The crowd gives a "wild whoop" when Jack rebukes Ralph, saying "Bollocks to the rules! We're strong ó we hunt! If there's a beast, we'll hunt it down! We'll close in and beat and beat and beat!" (p. 91). Clearly, the boys' fear of the beast and their ironic desire to kill it shows that the hold which society's rules once had over them has been loosened during the time they have spent without supervision on the island.

The evil within the boys has more effect on their existence as they spend more time on the island, isolated from the rest of society, and this decline is portrayed by Piggy's specs. Throughout the novel, Piggy represents the civilization and the rules from which the boys have been separated, and interestingly, as Piggy loses his ability to see, so do the other boys lose their vision of that civilization. When the story begins, Piggy can see clearly with both lenses of his spectacles intact, and the boys are still fairly civilized. For example, at one of their first meetings, the boys decide that they "can't have everybody talking at once" and that they "have to have ëHands up' like at school" (p. 33). However, after some time passes, the hunters become more concerned with slaughtering a pig than with being rescued and returning to civilization. When they return from a successful hunt in the jungle chanting "Kill the pig. Cut her throat. Spill her blood," Ralph and Piggy attempt to explain to the hunters that having meat for their meals is not as important as keeping the signal fire burning (p. 69). In an ensuing scuffle, Jack knocks Piggy specs from his face, smashing one of the lenses against the mountain rocks and greatly impairing his vision. Finally, after Jack forms his own tribe of savages, he and two of his followers ambush Ralph, Piggy, and Samneric, and in the midst of "a vicious snarling in the mouth of the shelter and the plunge and thump of living things," Piggy's specs are stolen, leaving him virtually blind (p. 167). Meanwhile, Jack returns to Castle Rock, "trotting steadily, exulting in his achievement," as he has practically abandoned all ties to civilized life (p. 168).

The story's setting presents two more symbols that assist in showing the decline of civility on the island. A majority of the island is taken up by the jungle, which is used by many authors as an archetype to represent death and decay. In fact, since the jungle is the lair of the beast, it, too, symbolizes the darkness naturally present within humans that is capable of ruling their lives. This evil eventually spreads to almost every boy on the island, just as in the jungle, "darkness poured out, submerging the ways between the trees till they were dim and strange as the bottom of the sea" (p. 57). At one end of the island, where the plane carrying the boys most likely crashed, there is a "long scar smashed into the jungle" (p. 1). While Golding does not include a large amount of description about the scar, the image of "broken trunks" with "jagged edges" is sufficient to give the reader an idea of the destruction caused to the island (p. 1, 2). Symbolically, this scar represents the destruction that man is naturally capable of causing and can be related to the harm the boys ultimately cause to one another, including the deaths of three boys, before they are rescued.

The degeneration of the boys' way of life is also very evident through the symbolic masks. When concealed by masks of clay paint, the hunters, especially Ralph, seem to have new personalities as they forget the taboos of society that once restrained them from giving in to their natural urges. For example, when Jack first paints his face to his satisfaction, he suddenly becomes a new, savage person. "He began to dance and his laughter became a bloodthirsty snarling. He capered toward Bill, and the mask was a thing of its own, behind which Jack hid, liberated from shame and self-consciousness" (p. 64). Certainly, Jack would not have acted in such a way if he had been in his home society, but behind the mask of paint, Jack feels free to act like a savage. It is also noteworthy, that the first mask that Jack creates is red, white, and black. These colors archetypically symbolize violence, terror, and evil, respectively, and in this novel, Golding uses these colors to illustrate those characteristics that are inherently present in humans.

The feeling of liberation that results from wearing the masks allows many of the boys to participate in the barbaric, inhumane pig hunts. Those hunts can be interpreted as symbolizing the boys' primal urges or even anarchy. In fact, many of the boys become so engulfed in their quest for the blood of a pig that they seem to forget about their hopes of returning to civilization and neglect to keep the signal fire burning. When Ralph tries to explain how important the signal fire is, Jack and the other hunters are still occupied with thoughts of the successful, gruesome hunt in which they just participated. "ëThere was lashings of blood,' said Jack, laughing and shuddering, ëyou should have seen it!'" (p. 69). Also, during a later celebration over another successful hunt, the boys become carried away while reenacting the slaughter. However, the boys have become so much like savages that they are unable to control themselves, and for a moment, they mistake Simon for the beast. "The sticks fell and the mouth of the circle crunched and screamed. The beast was on its knees in the center, its arm folded over its face" (p. 152). As a result of their uncontrolled urges, the boys soon kill one of their own.

Finally, one of the most memorable symbols that is used to show the violence and darkness which comes to rule life on the island is the rock, which Roger releases to kill Piggy. As an archetype in literature, a rock can symbolize strength and power, and since this rock is red, it also represents violence. It is Roger who feels strong and powerful as he stands on the ledge above Piggy. "High overhead, Roger, with a sense of delirium abandonment, leaned all his weight on the lever" (p. 180). When the rock lands below, it not only strikes Piggy, but it also shatters the conch shell. Up to that point, Piggy and the conch had been two of the few representations of civilization and common sense on the island. However, when the rock causes both of these to cease to exist, all order on the island is brought to an end, and the boys, who express no regrets over the death of Piggy, have fully become savages.

In conclusion, Lord of the Flies is a story that portrays the dark, deteriorating life that results from mankind's inherent capacity for evil, which is allowed to control humans when they are freed from the rules of society. Throughout the novel, Golding uses many different objects as symbols to illustrate this theme. Some of those objects would be insignificant in real life and would most likely be taken for granted. However, in Lord of the Flies, each of the previously mentioned symbols is vital to the story's theme.

Quiz 1

1. **Ralph uses what to summon the other boys?**
    A. a whistle
    B. a bell
    C. a fire
    D. a conch shell

2. **Piggy suffers from what?**
    A. asthma
    B. diabetes
    C. insomnia
    D. blindness

3. **Jack and his "hunters" are actually what type of group?**
    A. football team
    B. juvenile delinquents
    C. military school cadets
    D. choir

4. **The boys are stranded on an island where?**
    A. the Indian Ocean
    B. the Caribbean Sea
    C. the Pacific Ocean
    D. the North Atlantic

5. **Who identifies the island as part of a Coral Reef?**
    A. Jack
    B. Ralph
    C. Piggy
    D. Simon

6. **"Samneric" refers to what or whom?**
    A. the twins
    B. the island
    C. the youngest boys
    D. the Lord of the Flies

7. **"Creepers" refers to what?**
    A. snakes
    B. insects
    C. vines
    D. worms

8. **Ralph's father is what?**
    A. an advisor to Queen Elizabeth
    B. an officer in the English navy
    C. a pilot in the English air force
    D. a cartographer for the Scottish coast guard

9. **Piggy's real name is actually what?**
    A. Leslie
    B. Percival
    C. Gerald
    D. none of the above

10. **Why do Jack and his hunters attack Ralph and Piggy?**
    A. They want to intimidate them into joining their tribe.
    B. They want to steal the conch.
    C. They want to take control over the fire.
    D. They want to steal Piggy's glasses.

11. **What is referred to in the line, "There was lightning and thunder and rain. We was scared!"**
    A. Simon's murder
    B. Finding the beast
    C. The first day on the island
    D. Jack and his hunters

12. **Which character pretends to be a pig during the chant?**
    A. Maurice
    B. Eric
    C. Roger
    D. Simon

13. **According to Eric, what would be preferable to capture by Jack and his tribe?**
    A. facing the beast
    B. never leaving the jungle
    C. capture by the Reds
    D. starvation

14. **Which character repeats the saying, "Sucks to your ass-mar"?**
    A. Jack
    B. Ralph
    C. Roger
    D. Simon

15. **Who worries that the other boys think that he is insane?**
    A. Percival
    B. Jack
    C. Piggy
    D. Simon

16. **Who hesitates when the boys vote for chief, unsure whether to support Ralph?**
    A. Jack
    B. Roger
    C. Piggy
    D. Simon

17. **Ralph considers _____ the most important thing on the island.**
    A. the fire
    B. the conch
    C. food
    D. avoiding the beast

18. **Which of the following characters is not held as a prisoner by Jack and his hunters?**
    A. Wilfred
    B. Sam
    C. Eric
    D. Piggy

19. **All of the following are locations on the island except which?**
    A. the scar
    B. the lagoon
    C. Castle Rock
    D. the volcano

20. **Jack jokes that they could actually kill _____ in place of a pig during their dance.**
    A. a "littlun"
    B. Ralph
    C. Piggy
    D. Simon

21. **The conch shell can symbolize all of the following <i>except</i>:**
    A. democracy
    B. authority
    C. authoritarianism
    D. order

22. **Which of the following characters has the strongest religious sensibility?**
    A. Samneric
    B. Jack
    C. Piggy
    D. Simon

23. **Which of the following is a direct Satanic symbol?**
    A. Percival
    B. The pilot
    C. The spear sharpened at both ends
    D. The pig's head

24. **Which event in human history does not have a direct parallel in Lord of the Flies?**
    A. the discovery of fire
    B. the development of private property
    C. the development of government
    D. the move away from hunter-gatherer societies

25. **Ralph best represents which aspect of human nature?**
    A. spirituality
    B. instinct
    C. intellect
    D. moral choice

Quiz 1 Answer Key

1. **(D)** a conch shell
2. **(A)** asthma
3. **(D)** choir
4. **(C)** the Pacific Ocean
5. **(B)** Ralph
6. **(A)** the twins
7. **(C)** vines
8. **(B)** an officer in the English navy
9. **(D)** none of the above
10. **(D)** They want to steal Piggy's glasses.
11. **(A)** Simon's murder
12. **(C)** Roger
13. **(C)** capture by the Reds
14. **(B)** Ralph
15. **(D)** Simon
16. **(C)** Piggy
17. **(A)** the fire
18. **(D)** Piggy
19. **(D)** the volcano
20. **(A)** a "littlun"
21. **(C)** authoritarianism
22. **(D)** Simon
23. **(D)** The pig's head
24. **(D)** the move away from hunter-gatherer societies
25. **(D)** moral choice

Quiz 2

1. **Which of the following least represents Jack's political philosophy as leader?**
   A. anarchy
   B. communism
   C. totalitarianism
   D. militarism

2. **Which of the following does not represent civilized society?**
   A. fire on the mountain
   B. spear sharpened at both ends
   C. Piggy's glasses
   D. conch shell

3. **The descent from society into barbarism can be seen in all of the following symbols except _____**
   A. face painting
   B. Jack's clothing
   C. Piggy's glasses
   D. the fire on the mountain

4. **Piggy is best represented by which of the following objects?**
   A. glasses
   B. face paint
   C. candle-buds
   D. conch shell

5. **The boys' views of the beast suggest all of the following except _____**
   A. violence
   B. fear
   C. evil
   D. sloth

6. **Ralph symbolizes all of the following except _____**
   A. religiosity
   B. civilization
   C. rule of law
   D. moral choice

7. **The "littluns" best represent which aspect of society?**
    A. the intelligentsia
    B. the weak
    C. the ruling class
    D. the military

8. **Which of the following is the best implication of the Navy cruiser?**
    A. The Navy cruiser is a symbol of the boys' war.
    B. The Navy cruiser represents Ralph's father.
    C. The Navy cruiser returns the boys to a state of innocence.
    D. The Navy cruiser represents human technological progress.

9. **Which of the following does not represent evil in some form in Lord of the Flies?**
    A. Samneric
    B. Jack
    C. Roger
    D. the pig's head

10. **Which character best represents an adult sensibility?**
    A. Ralph
    B. Roger
    C. Piggy
    D. Simon

11. **"There's nothing in it of course. Just a feeling. But you can feel as if you're not hunting, but being hunted, as if something's behind you all the time in the jungle." Which is the best interpretation of this statement?**
    A. The only real threat to Jack is not another beast but his own suspicion and paranoia.
    B. Despite the lack of adult authority on the island, the boys cannot hide the consequences of their actions.
    C. Ralph suspects that he is being hunted by Jack and his choir.
    D. There is an unseen beast on the island that threaten the boys.

12. **Which quote best illustrates Simon's sensibility?**
    A. "The greatest ideas are the simplest. Now there was something to be done they worked with passion."
    B. "His mind was crowded with memories; memories of the knowledge that had come to them when they closed in on the struggling pig, knowledge that they had outwitted a living thing."
    C. "He obeyed an instinct that he did not know he possessed and swerved over the open space."
    D. "Evening was advancing toward the island; the sounds of bright fantastic birds, the bee-sounds, even the crying of the gulls that were

returning to their roosts among the square rocks, were fainter."

13. **Which statement by the Lord of the Flies best relates to Golding's view of the nature of evil?**
    A. "There isn't anyone to help you. Only me. And I'm the Beast."
    B. "You're not wanted. Understand? We are going to have fun on the island."
    C. "You knew, didn't you? I'm part of you?"
    D. "You are a silly little boy, just an ignorant, silly little boy."

14. **Before he dies, Piggy asks "Which is better: to have rules and agree, or to hunt and kill?" Which of the events of the book does not illustrate this theme?**
    A. Jack forms his own society apart from Ralph.
    B. Simon leaves the others to travel alone in the jungle.
    C. A ship passes by the island.
    D. Ralph and Simon struggle to build the shelters.

15. **"I should have thought that a pack of British boys would have been able to put up a better show than that" relates to which theme of the novel?**
    A. human instinct
    B. the nature of evil
    C. the clash between civilization and savagery
    D. the need for parental authority

16. **"Grownups know things. They ain't afraid of the dark. They'd meet and have tea and discuss. Then things 'ud be all right." This line deals with all of the following themes except:**
    A. sovereign restraint on behavior
    B. need for order
    C. inherent violence in human nature
    D. fear of the unknown

17. **Which of the following best illustrates the maxim, "the only thing we have to fear is fear itself"?**
    A. the conch shell
    B. the pilot
    C. the pig's head
    D. the shelters

18. **Based on the events and tone of the novel, which word best describes Golding's approach to humanity?**
    A. cynical
    B. hopeful
    C. skeptical
    D. idealistic

19. **"These painted savages would go further and further. Then there was that indefinable connection between himself and Jack; who would therefore never let him alone; never." Which interpretation best describes the significance of this quotation?**

    A. Golding constructs this passage as a definition of good and evil. Jack and Ralph are connected to one another because the "good" Ralph needs "evil" Jack to define him.

    B. Evil and violence will always conquer order and justice, for Jack has no rules or morals he must obey.

    C. This passage is in part a metaphor. Jack will never let Ralph alone because the evil within Jack is present within Ralph, as well as within all humanity.

    D. Because Jack and Ralph are brothers, they cannot bring themselves to ignore one another.

20. **The death of Simon illustrates all of the following themes except:**

    A. the boys are the agents of their own destruction

    B. humans act on violent instincts that they cannot control

    C. violence is a product of one's upbringing in society

    D. fear of the unknown causes greater danger than the unknown itself

21. **What is the best interpretation of Jack's inability to kill the pig at the beginning of the novel?**

    A. Power corrupts. Jack will be able to kill as soon as he gains authority over the other boys.

    B. The pig escapes because it is more afraid of Jack than Jack is of killing the pig.

    C. Jack obeys societal rules and regulations that discourage violence.

    D. Jack is only an innocent boy who must learn to become violent.

22. **Golding uses _____ several times to illustrate the thin line between man and beast.**

    A. Maurice

    B. Samneric

    C. Percival

    D. Roger

23. **Which of the following quotations best represents Golding's interpretation of the events of Lord of the Flies?**

    A. "Ralph wept for the end of innocence, the darkness of man's heart, and the fall through the air of the true, wise friend called Piggy."

    B. "I should have thought that a pack of British boys would have been able to put up a better show than that."

    C. "Bathing. That's the only thing to do."

    D. "Of course we're frightened sometimes but we put up with being frightened. As for the fear--you'll have to put up with that like the rest of us."

24. **All of the following demonstrate the theme that human society requires communal effort and consideration except** _____
    A. the hunt for the beast
    B. building the shelters
    C. tending the fire
    D. Ralph's rules for the lavatory

25. **The murder of Simon demonstrates Golding's view that human violence is:**
    A. a quality particular to the British
    B. learned from experience
    C. preventable
    D. instinctive

Quiz 2 Answer Key

1. **(B)** communism
2. **(B)** spear sharpened at both ends
3. **(D)** the fire on the mountain
4. **(A)** glasses
5. **(D)** sloth
6. **(A)** religiosity
7. **(B)** the weak
8. **(A)** The Navy cruiser is a symbol of the boys' war.
9. **(A)** Samneric
10. **(C)** Piggy
11. **(A)** The only real threat to Jack is not another beast but his own suspicion and paranoia.
12. **(D)** "Evening was advancing toward the island; the sounds of bright fantastic birds, the bee-sounds, even the crying of the gulls that were returning to their roosts among the square rocks, were fainter."
13. **(C)** "You knew, didn't you? I'm part of you?"
14. **(B)** Simon leaves the others to travel alone in the jungle.
15. **(C)** the clash between civilization and savagery
16. **(C)** inherent violence in human nature
17. **(B)** the pilot
18. **(A)** cynical
19. **(C)** This passage is in part a metaphor. Jack will never let Ralph alone because the evil within Jack is present within Ralph, as well as within all humanity.
20. **(C)** violence is a product of one's upbringing in society
21. **(C)** Jack obeys societal rules and regulations that discourage violence.
22. **(A)** Maurice
23. **(A)** "Ralph wept for the end of innocence, the darkness of man's heart, and the fall through the air of the true, wise friend called Piggy."
24. **(A)** the hunt for the beast
25. **(D)** instinctive

Quiz 3

1. **The "scar" on the island refers to what?**
    A. the wreckage from the crashed plane
    B. the lagoon
    C. the bodies of the crash victims
    D. a deep crater in the ground

2. **Piggy suggests to Ralph that they make a list of** _____
    A. the dead
    B. supplies
    C. things to do
    D. names

3. **Piggy's aunt does what?**
    A. operates an animal shelter
    B. curates an art gallery
    C. works for a conservative think tank
    D. owns a candy store

4. **The boys are from** _____
    A. the Motherland
    B. the Home Counties
    C. the Home Countries
    D. the Homeland

5. **Upon first hearing it, Jack thinks the conch shell is a** _____
    A. whistle
    B. trumpet
    C. megaphone
    D. horn

6. **The island is shaped like what?**
    A. a train
    B. a boat
    C. a fish
    D. an ear

7. **Simon suggests that the boys make a map of the island. On what does he suggest they draw it?**
    A. palm leaf
    B. bark
    C. shell
    D. cloth

8. **Water is served in _____**
    A. a coconut shell
    B. a pig's skull
    C. a conch shell
    D. a human skull

9. **The "littluns" are afraid of a "beastie," which they describe as a _____**
    A. forest-creature
    B. snake-thing
    C. pig-monster
    D. politician

10. **Who are the smallest boys on the island?**
    A. Percival and Maurice
    B. Johnny and Henry
    C. Maurice and Johnny
    D. Percival and Johnny

11. **Jack rejects the conch shell in which chapter of Lord of the Flies?**
    A. Chapter Eight
    B. Chapter One
    C. Chapter Ten
    D. Chapter Six

12. **Who is the only boy on the island who does not believe in ghosts?**
    A. Percival
    B. Jack
    C. Ralph
    D. Piggy

13. **Of which sea animal is Percival afraid?**
    A. anemone
    B. whale
    C. shark
    D. squid

14. **Piggy wants to build what in the sand?**
    A. sundial
    B. pig trap
    C. Castle Rock
    D. well

15. **In Chapter Four, which character notices that the fire has gone out?**
    A. Maurice
    B. Jack
    C. Ralph
    D. Piggy

16. **Which of the following is NOT a feature of the littluns' sandcastles?**
    A. marks
    B. walls
    C. moats
    D. train tracks

17. **The "littluns" eat mostly _____**
    A. pig meat
    B. fish
    C. nuts
    D. fruit

18. **To which mythological figure is the dead parachutist an allusion?**
    A. Lucifer
    B. Orpheus
    C. God
    D. Juno

19. **Jack attributes his lack of success in hunting to what factor?**
    A. his hunters did not help him
    B. his spear was too short
    C. the animals could see him
    D. the animals could hear him

20. **To whom does Jack deny pig-meat?**
    A. Ralph
    B. Roger
    C. Piggy
    D. Henry

21. **Simon's body is surrounded by what?**
    A. seaweed
    B. plane wreckage
    C. turtles
    D. fish

22. **What happens to the body of the parachutist?**
    A. tumbles into the fire
    B. blown away by the wind
    C. dragged away by the ocean tide
    D. comes alive

23. **At the feast, the adorned Jack is compared to what?**
    A. an idol
    B. an angel
    C. a soldier
    D. God

24. **Simon's confrontation with the Lord of the Flies evokes which biblical story?**
    A. The prodigal son returning
    B. The trials of Job
    C. Christ's meeting Satan after forty days in the wilderness
    D. The Annunciation

25. **The storm following the feast represents what?**
 A. the boys' homesickness
 B. the end of the war in the Home Counties
 C. the corruption of Piggy
 D. the chaos and anarchy of Jack's society

Quiz 3 Answer Key

1. **(A)** the wreckage from the crashed plane
2. **(D)** names
3. **(D)** owns a candy store
4. **(B)** the Home Counties
5. **(B)** trumpet
6. **(B)** a boat
7. **(B)** bark
8. **(A)** a coconut shell
9. **(B)** snake-thing
10. **(D)** Percival and Johnny
11. **(D)** Chapter Six
12. **(D)** Piggy
13. **(D)** squid
14. **(A)** sundial
15. **(D)** Piggy
16. **(C)** moats
17. **(D)** fruit
18. **(A)** Lucifer
19. **(C)** the animals could see him
20. **(C)** Piggy
21. **(D)** fish
22. **(B)** blown away by the wind
23. **(A)** an idol
24. **(C)** Christ's meeting Satan after forty days in the wilderness
25. **(D)** the chaos and anarchy of Jack's society

Quiz 4

1. **Which of the following does Jack NOT promise his tribesmen?**
   A. rescue
   B. pig meat
   C. protection
   D. Funding socialist causes

2. **To which of the following books does Lord of the Flies NOT allude?**
   A. The Bible
   B. Jane Eyre
   C. The Coral Island
   D. Heart of Darkness

3. **Upon seeing the dead parachutist, Ralph compares it to what?**
   A. a squid
   B. an angel
   C. a great ape
   D. a wild boar

4. **Who first spots the "beast"?**
   A. Samneric
   B. Jack
   C. Roger
   D. Simon

5. **While searching for the beast, the boys find what on an unexplored side of the mountain?**
   A. a river
   B. caves
   C. goats
   D. fruit

6. **Golding draws on negative stereotypes of what culture to characterize the savagery of Jack's tribe?**
   A. Chinese
   B. Russian
   C. Japanese
   D. Aboriginal

7. **In "Gift for the Darkness," Ralph's and Piggy's fire goes out. According to Piggy, what is the cause?**
   A. there are no longer enough boys to tend it
   B. the beast
   C. the rainy season
   D. there is no more firewood

8. **Who calls the pig's head on the stick the Lord of the Flies?**
   A. Samneric
   B. Jack
   C. Ralph
   D. Simon

9. **The slaughter of the sow resembles what?**
   A. an atomic explosion
   B. the storm
   C. rape
   D. the Passion of Jesus

10. **In which chapter does Simon die?**
    A. Gift for the Darkness
    B. A View to a Death
    C. Shadows and Tall Trees
    D. Beast from Water

11. **Why is the pig's head called the Lord of the Flies?**
    A. like the beast, it flies
    B. it is an offering to the vicious flies on the island
    C. it attracts flies
    D. no one knows

12. **Chapter Eight is called "Gift for the Darkness." What is the gift?**
    A. the beast
    B. a littlun
    C. the new signal fire
    D. the Lord of the Flies

13. **On their excusion to find the beast, what convinces Ralph that they will not be rescued?**
    A. the beast
    B. Jack's increasingly violent behavior
    C. the impenetrability of the ocean tide
    D. the vastness of the island

14. **When the boys are first stranded, how does Ralph think the group will be rescued?**
    A. a passing helicopter will spot them
    B. he spots a lighthouse on the horizon
    C. he knows how to build a raft, and they will sail
    D. his father will find them by ship

15. **On the search for the beast, the boys spot a boar. Who throws the first spear?**
    A. Maurice
    B. Jack
    C. Ralph
    D. Roger

16. **Why does Jack set the forest on fire?**
    A. to smoke Ralph out of hiding
    B. to create more clearing space
    C. to smoke the beast out of hiding
    D. to attract a passing ship

17. **What do Jack and his hunters steal from Ralph's camp?**
    A. Piggy's glasses
    B. Samneric
    C. the conch
    D. firewood

18. **What does Jack order his hunters to do to Samneric?**
    A. torture them
    B. kill them
    C. paint them
    D. tie them up

19. **Who kills Piggy?**
    A. Jack
    B. Bill
    C. Ralph
    D. Roger

20. **When Ralph finds Samneric at Jack's camp, what are they doing?**
    A. dancing and chanting
    B. eating pig meat
    C. being tortured by Jack
    D. guarding the entrance

21. **What attracts the navy cruiser to the island?**
    A. Jack's chanting
    B. the signal fire
    C. the forest fire
    D. the beast

22. **When he travels to Jack's camp following Piggy's murder, what does Ralph use as a spear?**
    A. the stick from the Lord of the Flies
    B. a small log
    C. a piece of firewood
    D. a stick he stole from Roger

23. **The navy officer compares the boys' early days on the island to what?**
    A. The Coral Island
    B. Treasure Island
    C. The Garden of Eden
    D. Heart of Darkness

24. **The navy officer claims that who or what should always be organized?**
    A. the Americans
    B. soldiers
    C. choir boys
    D. the British

25. **Why does the navy officer turn away from the boys when they start to cry?**
  A. he is sad
  B. he is disgusted
  C. he is distracted
  D. he is embarrassed

Quiz 4 Answer Key

1. **(A)** rescue
2. **(B)** Jane Eyre
3. **(C)** a great ape
4. **(A)** Samneric
5. **(B)** caves
6. **(D)** Aboriginal
7. **(A)** there are no longer enough boys to tend it
8. **(D)** Simon
9. **(C)** rape
10. **(B)** A View to a Death
11. **(C)** it attracts flies
12. **(D)** the Lord of the Flies
13. **(C)** the impenetrability of the ocean tide
14. **(D)** his father will find them by ship
15. **(C)** Ralph
16. **(A)** to smoke Ralph out of hiding
17. **(A)** Piggy's glasses
18. **(D)** tie them up
19. **(D)** Roger
20. **(D)** guarding the entrance
21. **(C)** the forest fire
22. **(A)** the stick from the Lord of the Flies
23. **(A)** The Coral Island
24. **(D)** the British
25. **(D)** he is embarrassed

ClassicNotes

GradeSaver™

Getting you the grade since 1999™

ClassicNotes

GradeSaver™

Getting you the grade since 1999™

Other ClassicNotes from GradeSaver™

The English Patient
Ethan Frome
The Eumenides
Everything is Illuminated
Fahrenheit 451
The Fall of the House of
   Usher
Farewell to Arms
The Federalist Papers
For Whom the Bell Tolls
The Fountainhead
Frankenstein
Franny and Zooey
Glass Menagerie
The God of Small Things
The Good Earth
The Grapes of Wrath
Great Expectations
The Great Gatsby
The Guest
Hamlet
The Handmaid's Tale
Hard Times
Heart of Darkness
Hedda Gabler
Henry IV (Pirandello)
Henry IV Part 1
Henry IV Part 2
Henry V
Herzog
The Hobbit
Homo Faber
House of Mirth
House of the Seven
   Gables
The House of the Spirits

House on Mango Street
Howards End
A Hunger Artist
I Know Why the Caged
   Bird Sings
An Ideal Husband
Iliad
The Importance of Being
   Earnest
In Our Time
Inherit the Wind
Invisible Man
The Island of Dr. Moreau
Jane Eyre
Jazz
The Jew of Malta
The Joy Luck Club
Julius Caesar
Jungle of Cities
Kama Sutra
Kidnapped
King Lear
Last of the Mohicans
Leviathan
Libation Bearers
Life is Beautiful
The Lion, the Witch and
   the Wardrobe
Lolita
Long Day's Journey Into
   Night
Lord Jim
Lord of the Flies
The Lord of the Rings:
   The Fellowship of the
   Ring

The Lord of the Rings:
   The Return of the
   King
The Lord of the Rings:
   The Two Towers
A Lost Lady
Love in the Time of
   Cholera
The Love Song of J.
   Alfred Prufrock
Lucy
Macbeth
Madame Bovary
Manhattan Transfer
Mansfield Park
MAUS
The Mayor of
   Casterbridge
Measure for Measure
Medea
Merchant of Venice
Metamorphoses
The Metamorphosis
Middlemarch
Midsummer Night's
   Dream
Moby Dick
Moll Flanders
Mother Courage and Her
   Children
Mrs. Dalloway
Much Ado About
   Nothing
My Antonia
Native Son
Night

For our full list of over 250 Study Guides, Quizzes,
Sample College Application Essays, Literature Essays and E-texts, visit:

www.gradesaver.com

ClassicNotes

Getting you the grade since 1999™

ClassicNotes

GradeSaver™

Getting you the grade since 1999™

Other ClassicNotes from GradeSaver™

The English Patient
Ethan Frome
The Eumenides
Everything is Illuminated
Fahrenheit 451
The Fall of the House of
    Usher
Farewell to Arms
The Federalist Papers
For Whom the Bell Tolls
The Fountainhead
Frankenstein
Franny and Zooey
Glass Menagerie
The God of Small Things
The Good Earth
The Grapes of Wrath
Great Expectations
The Great Gatsby
The Guest
Hamlet
The Handmaid's Tale
Hard Times
Heart of Darkness
Hedda Gabler
Henry IV (Pirandello)
Henry IV Part 1
Henry IV Part 2
Henry V
Herzog
The Hobbit
Homo Faber
House of Mirth
House of the Seven
    Gables
The House of the Spirits

House on Mango Street
Howards End
A Hunger Artist
I Know Why the Caged
    Bird Sings
An Ideal Husband
Iliad
The Importance of Being
    Earnest
In Our Time
Inherit the Wind
Invisible Man
The Island of Dr. Moreau
Jane Eyre
Jazz
The Jew of Malta
The Joy Luck Club
Julius Caesar
Jungle of Cities
Kama Sutra
Kidnapped
King Lear
Last of the Mohicans
Leviathan
Libation Bearers
Life is Beautiful
The Lion, the Witch and
    the Wardrobe
Lolita
Long Day's Journey Into
    Night
Lord Jim
Lord of the Flies
The Lord of the Rings:
    The Fellowship of the
    Ring

The Lord of the Rings:
    The Return of the
    King
The Lord of the Rings:
    The Two Towers
A Lost Lady
Love in the Time of
    Cholera
The Love Song of J.
    Alfred Prufrock
Lucy
Macbeth
Madame Bovary
Manhattan Transfer
Mansfield Park
MAUS
The Mayor of
    Casterbridge
Measure for Measure
Medea
Merchant of Venice
Metamorphoses
The Metamorphosis
Middlemarch
Midsummer Night's
    Dream
Moby Dick
Moll Flanders
Mother Courage and Her
    Children
Mrs. Dalloway
Much Ado About
    Nothing
My Antonia
Native Son
Night

For our full list of over 250 Study Guides, Quizzes,
Sample College Application Essays, Literature Essays and E-texts, visit:

www.gradesaver.com

ClassicNotes

GradeSaver™

Getting you the grade since 1999™

Other ClassicNotes from GradeSaver™

No Exit
Notes from Underground
O Pioneers
The Odyssey
Oedipus Rex / Oedipus
    the King
Of Mice and Men
The Old Man and the Sea
On Liberty
On the Road
One Day in the Life of
    Ivan Denisovich
One Flew Over the
    Cuckoo's Nest
One Hundred Years of
    Solitude
Oroonoko
Othello
Our Town
Pale Fire
Paradise Lost
A Passage to India
The Pearl
The Picture of Dorian
    Gray
Poems of W.B. Yeats:
    The Rose
Portrait of the Artist as a
    Young Man
Pride and Prejudice
Prometheus Bound
Pudd'nhead Wilson
Pygmalion
Rabbit, Run
A Raisin in the Sun

The Real Life of
    Sebastian Knight
Red Badge of Courage
The Republic
Richard II
Richard III
The Rime of the Ancient
    Mariner
Robinson Crusoe
Roll of Thunder, Hear
    My Cry
Romeo and Juliet
A Room of One's Own
A Room With a View
Rosencrantz and
    Guildenstern Are
    Dead
Salome
The Scarlet Letter
The Scarlet Pimpernel
Secret Sharer
Sense and Sensibility
A Separate Peace
Shakespeare's Sonnets
Siddhartha
Silas Marner
Sir Gawain and the
    Green Knight
Sister Carrie
Six Characters in Search
    of an Author
Slaughterhouse Five
Snow Falling on Cedars
The Social Contract
Something Wicked This
    Way Comes

Song of Roland
Sons and Lovers
The Sorrows of Young
    Werther
The Sound and the Fury
Spring Awakening
The Stranger
A Streetcar Named
    Desire
The Sun Also Rises
Tale of Two Cities
The Taming of the Shrew
The Tempest
Tender is the Night
Tess of the D'Urbervilles
Their Eyes Were
    Watching God
Things Fall Apart
The Threepenny Opera
The Time Machine
Titus Andronicus
To Build a Fire
To Kill a Mockingbird
To the Lighthouse
Treasure Island
Troilus and Cressida
Turn of the Screw
Twelfth Night
Ulysses
Uncle Tom's Cabin
Utopia
A Very Old Man With
    Enormous Wings
The Visit
Volpone
Waiting for Godot

For our full list of over 250 Study Guides, Quizzes,
Sample College Application Essays, Literature Essays and E-texts, visit:

www.gradesaver.com

ClassicNotes

GradeSaver™

Getting you the grade since 1999™

Other ClassicNotes from GradeSaver™

Waiting for Lefty
Walden
Washington Square
Where the Red Fern
    Grows
White Fang
White Noise
White Teeth
Who's Afraid of Virginia
    Woolf
Wide Sargasso Sea
Winesburg, Ohio
The Winter's Tale
Woyzeck
Wuthering Heights
The Yellow Wallpaper
Yonnondio: From the
    Thirties

For our full list of over 250 Study Guides, Quizzes,
Sample College Application Essays, Literature Essays and E-texts, visit:

www.gradesaver.com

Made in the USA
San Bernardino, CA
19 August 2014